THE COMPLETE PRONUNCIATION COURSE

DYLANE MOREAU

TABLE OF CONTENTS

HOW TO USE THIS COURSE?

This course includes:

This book includes **55 video lessons** to master French pronunciation, and **105 recordings**.
The video lessons can be found at www.theperfectfrench.com/french-pronunciation-course
To access the recordings, go to www.theperfectfrench.com/pronunciation-course-audios
The Complete French Pronunciation Course will guide you and help you remember all the how's and why's of French pronunciation.
If you are feeling lost and don't know what to study next, you can get my free self-study guide here: www.theperfectfrench.com/free-guide

How to use this course and practice at home?

Watch each video-lesson to learn everything about the pronunciation of each sound and letter combination in French.

Listen multiple times to the recordings. Pronunciation is closely linked to your ability to hear the sound. Listening to them often will help you to hear the sound correctly to get the pronunciation right. "If you can't hear it, you can't pronounce it".

Practice your pronunciation like the recordings "Focus on *specific letter / sound*" followed by the " *Specific letter / sound* in words".
When you feel ready, record yourself and listen back-to-back to my recording and yours. This will give you the opportunity to practice alone and correct yourself if needed.

How to keep learning by yourself?

Check the pronunciation of a specific word:

Simply google "WORD pronunciation IPA" (IPA stands for "International Phonetic Alphabet). This search will bring you to the Wikipedia page of the said word. You will have the opportunity to look at its phonetic and use the player to listen to the word. If you don't need the IPA, you can also use google translate. The pronunciation is not always great but that will give you a general idea.

How to keep learning by yourself?

Practice listening and reading at the same time:

This solution isn't always the most affordable but if you are a book person, choose a book you like and buy the audiobook as well as the eBook or physical book. Listen to the audiobook and read at the same time.
This will train your ear to all the different sounds as well as train your brain to recognize the letters combination, silent letters, and links.
This will also give you the chance to learn new vocabulary.

Another method is to watch TV in French with French subtitles. This is always the last one I recommend because actors (or voice over) tend to speak fast and not always as clearly as an audiobook.

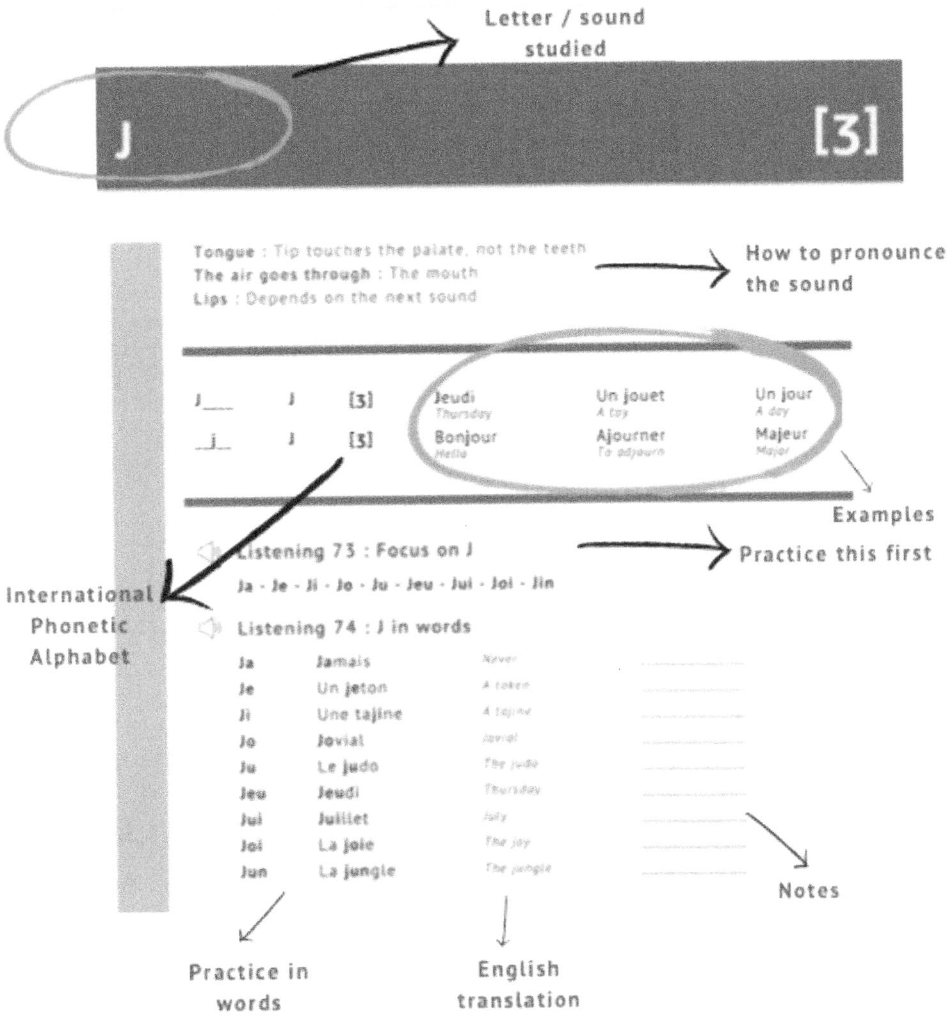

THE ALPHABET

A	Ah	**A**cheter	*To buy*
B	Bay	Un **b**onbon	*A candy*
C	Say	Une **c**arotte	*A carrot*
D	Day	Une **d**ent	*A tooth*
E		L**e**	*The*
F	Ef	Une **f**ête	*A party*
G	Jay	Un **g**arage	*A garage*
H	Ash	Un **h**ibou	*An owl*
I	Ee	Une **i**dée	*An idea*
J	Jee	**J**ouer	*To play*
K	Kah	Un **k**it	*A kit*
L	El	La **l**umière	*The light*
M	Em	**M**aman	*Mom*
N	En	**N**on	*No*
O	Oh	Un **o**bjet	*An object*
P	Pay	**P**our	*For*
Q	Ku	Une **q**ueue	*Tail*
R	Air	Un **r**at	*A rat*
S	Ess	Une **s**ouris	*A mouse*
T	Tay	Un **t**éléphone	*A phone*
U		**U**nir	*To unify*
V	Vay	**V**oir	*To see*
W	Doobl vay	Un **w**agon	*A train car*
X	Eeks	Un **x**ylophone	*A xylophone*
Y	Ee grek	Un **y**aourt	*A yaourt*
Z	Zed	Un **z**èbre	*A zebra*

Listening 1: The alphabet

A - B - C - D - E - F - G - H - I - J - K - L - M - N - O - P - Q - R - S - T - U - V - W - X - Y - Z

CARACTERISTICS

26 letters

20 consonants

6 vowels

THE VOWELS

A O

E U

I Y

THE ACCENTS

Accent aigu

Accent grave

Accent circonflexe

Tréma and C cédille

THE TYPES OF ACCENTS

ACCENT AIGU

ACCENT GRAVE

ACCENT CIRCONFLEXE

TRÉMA

CÉDILLE

Accents in French have very specific roles. In some cases, such as the letter E, the accents will radically change its pronunciation.

"**Accent aigu**" only appears on the letter E.

The "**accent grave**", except on E, is used to differentiate words with and without accent, without changing the pronunciation of the letter. We will look more into it in the next few pages.

The "**accent circonflexe**" and especially "Ê" indicates that the letter used to be followed by a S. We removed the S and added a ^.

The "**tréma**" specifically means that we have to pronounce the vowel distinctively.
And finally, the "**cédille**", simply sounds like a S.

ACCENT AIGU

"**Accent aigu**" or acute accent in English, is pronounced like "AY" in English but shorter.

Only used on the letter E.

Une **é**cole	*A school*
Écouter	*To listen*
Chant**é**	*Sang*
Une television	*A television*
Un telephone	*A phone*
Un canap**é**	*A couch*

Listening 2: Focus on É

Bé - Cé - Dé - Fé - Gé - Lé - Mé - Né - Pé - Ré - Sé - Té - Vé - Xé - Zé - Ché - Ié

Listening 3: É in words

Bé	Un **bébé**	*A baby*	________________
Cé	Une **cé**dille	*A cedilla*	________________
Dé	**Dé**cembre	*December*	________________
Fé	**Fé**vrier	*February*	________________
Gé	Chan**gé**	*Changed*	________________
Lé	**Lé**ger	*Light*	________________
Mé	**Mé**langé	*Mixed*	________________
Né	Me**né**	*Led*	________________
Pé	Une é**pé**e	*A sword*	________________
Ré	**Ré**pondre	*To answer*	________________
Sé	Ver**sé**	*Poured*	________________
Té	Chan**té**	*Sang*	________________
Vé	La**vé**	*Washed*	________________
Xé	Ve**xé**	*Upset*	________________
Zé	**Zé**ro	*Zero*	________________
Ché	**Ché**ri	*Darling*	________________
Ié	Pl**ié**	*Folded*	________________

ACCENT GRAVE

With À and Ù, the pronunciation of the letters and the words doesn't change.
We used the "**accent grave**" to differentiate some words such as :

à vs a	*To - Has*
L**à** vs la	*There - The*
O**ù** vs ou	*Where - Or*

À

L**à**	*There*
Voil**à**	*Here*
Déj**à**	*Already*

Ù

O**ù**	*Where*

But it changes the pronunciation of E = **È**.
It's pronounced like the ***AI*** in ***FAIR***, but shorter.

Le p**è**re	*The father*
La m**è**re	*The mother*
Fi**è**re	*Proud (f)*
Un mammif**è**re	*A mammal*
Tr**è**s	*Very*
Un z**è**bre	*A zebra*

ACCENT CIRCONFLEXE

Ê sounds exactly the same as **È** that we saw just before.
It's pronounced like the ***AI*** in ***FAIR***, but shorter.

Une f**ê**te	*A party*
Une t**ê**te	*A head*
Une fen**ê**tre	*A window*
La gr**ê**le	*The hail*
R**ê**ver	*To dream*
Être	*To be*

For **Â and Ô**, the official pronunciation is longer and softer than the letters without accent.
For **Î and Û**, depending where the language is spoken, it can be softer or stay the same as the letters without accent.

T**â**che vs Tache
P**â**te vs Patte

Une **â**me	*A soul*
Un ch**â**teau	*A castle*
G**â**cher	*To waste*
Avoir h**â**te	*Can't wait*
Une t**â**che	*A task*
La p**â**te	*The dough*

Une **î**le	*An island*
Le d**î**ner	*The dinner*
Le g**î**te	*The lodge*
Une bo**î**te	*A box*
Fra**î**che	*Fresh (f)*
Appara**î**tre	*To appear*

Un h**ô**tel	*An hotel*
T**ô**t	*Early*
Aussit**ô**t	*As soon as*
Le ch**ô**mage	*Unemployment*
Un imp**ô**t	*A tax*
Dr**ô**le	*Funny*

S**û**r	*Sure*
Un b**û**cheron	*A lumberjack*
Une b**û**che	*A log*
Ao**û**t	*August*

TRÉMA and CÉDILLE

The accent "**tréma**" indicates that the vowel has to be pronounced separately from the one immediately before it.
We used it on **ë - ï**.

Maïs vs Mais	*Corn vs But*

Noël	*Christmas*
Du maïs	*Some corn*
Un aïeul	*An ancestor*

The "**cédille**" is placed on the letter "**C**" and only if followed by one of the following letters: **A - O and U**.
It turns "**C**" into the sound "**S**".

Un Fran**ç**ais	*A French man*
Un gar**ç**on	*A boy*
Une fa**ç**ade	*A facade*
Un re**ç**u	*A receipt*

Notes :

HOW TO SPELL

Spelling in French is easy but there are a few rules to follow.

In case of an accent, you need to specify the accent:

É say "**E accent aigu**"
È say "**E accent grave**"
Ê say "**E accent circonflexe**"
Ï say "**I tréma**"
Ç say "**C cédille**"
...

In case of a double letter:

SS say "**Double S**"
PP say "**Double P**"
...

Try it:

1. François
2. Dylane
3. Stéfanie
4. Anaïs
5. Isabelle
6. William
7. Geneviève
8. Alexandra
9. Christopher
10. Christian

MUTE / SILENT LETTERS

E PRECEDED BY A VOWEL

E PRECEDED BY A CONSONANT

E IN THE MIDDLE OF THE WORD

LAST CONSONANT OF THE WORD

PLURAL OF WORDS

PLURAL OF VERBS

THE LETTER H

THE LETTER U

THE LETTER M

Mute letters, also called silent letters, is the pronunciation rule that confuse French learners the most. Some letters are important for grammar and spelling but don't change the pronunciation of the word itself.

They are usually at the end of the word with a few exceptions at the beginning and in the middle of the words.

MUTE / SILENT LETTERS

Let's start with the letter **E, the most common silent letter**.

We don't pronounce E when it's placed after the vowels:

1. IE = I

Une boug**ie**	*A candle*
La pharmac**ie**	*The pharmacy*
La librair**ie**	*The bookstore*

2. AIE = AI

La monn**aie**	*The change*
Une pl**aie**	*A wound*
Une r**aie**	*A ray*

3. UE = U

Une aven**ue**	*An avenue*
Bienven**ue**	*Welcome*
Une r**ue**	*A street*

4. OIE = OI

La j**oie**	*The joy*
La s**oie**	*The silk*
Une **oie**	*A goose*

5. OUE = OU

La b**oue**	*The mud*
La j**oue**	*The cheek*
La r**oue**	*The wheel*

6. EUE = EU

La banli**eue**	*The suburb*
La qu**eue**	*The tail*

If **E** is placed after **B - C - D - G - N - P - R - S - T**, we don't pronounce the **E** but we will pronounce the letter before:

1. BE = B

Une ro**be**	*A dress*
Un tu**be**	*A tube*
Un ver**be**	*A verb*

2. CE = C (S)

Une chan**ce**	*A chance*
Une lan**ce**	*A spear*
Une ron**ce**	*A thorn*

2. DE = D

Chau**de**	*Hot (f)*
Froi**de**	*Cold (f)*
Une bala**de**	*A walk*

4. GE = G (J)

Je chan**ge**	*I am changing*
Un lan**ge**	*A diaper*
Je man**ge**	*I am eating*

MUTE / SILENT LETTERS

5. NE = N

Une semai**ne** *A week*
Fémini**ne** *Feminine*
Un télépho**ne** *A phone*

4. RE = R

Un laboratoi**re** *A laboratory*
Une coiffu**re** *A haircut*
La ga**re** *The train station*

6. TE = T

Une fê**te** *A party*
Une tê**te** *A head*
Une carot**te** *A carrot*

2. PE = P

La cou**pe** *The cut*
Une pi**pe** *A pipe*
Une ju**pe** *A skirt*

4. SE = S (Z)

Une chai**se** *A chair*
Une entrepri**se** *A company*
Une vali**se** *A luggage*

E can also be silent in the middle of the word:

Un pai**e**ment *A payment*
Un remerci**e**ment *A thank you*
Une prom**e**nade *A walk*

But **E** is pronounced in articles and small words:

D**e** – L**e** – M**e** – J**e** – T**e** – Qu**e** – C**e** – N**e** - ...

MUTE / SILENT LETTERS

We don't pronounce the last letter of the word if it's:

1. B (exception)

Le plom**b** — *The lead*

5. D

Le ni**d** — *The nest*
Sour**d** — *Deaf*

7. G

Le poin**g** — *The fist*
Excluding English words: smoking, camping, ...

3. P

Beaucou**p** — *A lot*
Tro**p** — *Too many / Too much*

4. T

L'ar**t** — *The art*
Le concer**t** — *The concert*
Un desser**t** — *A dessert*

5. Z

Le ne**z** — *The nose*
Che**z** — *At*
Du ri**z** — *Some rice*

2. C

Un ban**c** — *A bench*
Blan**c** — *White*

4. F after a consonant

Un cer**f** — *A deer*
Le ner**f** — *The nerve*

6. L

Un outi**l** — *A tool*
Un fusi**l** — *A gun*

2. S

Un bra**s** — *An arm*
Le repo**s** — *The rest*

4. X

Un choi**x** — *A choice*
Une croi**x** — *A cross*
Deu**x** — *Two*

MUTE / SILENT LETTERS

We don't pronounce the last letter of words such as **S** and **X**:

Un chien => Des chien**s**	*A dog => Dogs*
Un téléphone => Des téléphone**s**	*A phone => Phones*
Une table => Des table**s**	*A table => Tables*
Un hibou => Des hibou**x**	*An owl => Owls*
Un gâteau => Des gâteau**x**	*A cake => Cakes*
Un cheveu => Des cheveu**x**	*A hair => Hair*

We don't pronounce the plural of verbs -**ENT**:

Il chante => Ils chant**ent**	*He sings => They sing*
Il mange => Ils mang**ent**	*He eats => They eat*
Elle dort => Elles dorm**ent**	*She sleeps => They sleep*

We don't pronounce the letter **H in French, at the beginning and in the middle of a word**:

Un **h**ibou	*An owl*	Un vé**h**icule	*A vehicle*
Un **h**éros	*A hero*	Un tra**h**ison	*A betrayal*
Une **h**aie	*A hedge*		

We don't pronounce the letter **U when preceded by Q or G**:

Une q**u**eue	*A tail*	Long**u**e	*Long (f)*
Un q**u**art	*A quarter*	Une lang**u**e	*A tongue*

We don't pronounce the letter **M** in these specific words:

L'auto**m**ne	*Fall / Autumn*
Conda**m**ner	*To convict*

*and variations

CONTRACTIONS

Contractions or "**Élisions**" in French, happen when a noun, a verb or a preposition start with a vowel or a h muet (see more about this subject at H).
They are important to keep a good flow of pronunciation.

They happen with:

The definite articles **LE** and **LA**:

LE = L'

Le avocat	**L'a**vocat	*The avocado / lawyer*
Le arbre	**L'a**rbre	*The tree*

LA = L'

La école	**L'é**cole	*The school*
La orange	**L'o**range	*The orange*

The direct object pronouns – **DOP**:

Je le emporte	Je **l'e**mporte	*I take it*
Tu le assures	Tu **l'a**ssures	*You insure it*
Il la envoie	Il **l'e**nvoie	*He sends it*

With **2 letters words**:

Ce	Ce + est	**C'e**st	*This is / It is*
De	De + autre	**D'a**utre	*Other*
Je	Je + ai	**J'a**i	*I have*
Ne	Il ne + aime pas	Il **n'a**ime pas	*He doesn't like*
Se	Il se + arrange	Il **s'a**rrange	*He arranges himself*

Que and variations:

Que	Que + est	**Qu'i**l	*That he*
Jusque	Jusque + à	Jusq**u'à**	*Until*
Lorsque	Lorsque + elle	Lorsq**u'e**lle	*When she*
Puisque	Puisque + on	Puisq**u'o**n	*Since we*

LINKS

"**Liaisons**" in French happen when a word ends with a consonant (usually silent) and is followed by a word starting with a vowel. Therefore, the sound of the consonant is transferred to the second word.

There are 6 different sounds with liaisons: **Z, T, N, V, K and R**

S – **X** - **Z** + vowel make the sound **Z**:

Vous avez	Vou **z**avez	*You have*
Trois enfants	Troi **z**enfants	*Three children*
Deux ans	Deu **z**ans	*Two years*
Dix oiseaux	Di **z**oiseux	*Two birds*
Chez elle	Chez **z**elle	*At hers*
Chez eux	Chez **z**eux	*At theirs*

D – **T** + vowel make the sound **T** :

Un grand arbre	Un gran **t**arbre	*A tall tree*
Un petit insecte	Un peti **t**insecte	*A small insect*
Il est à	Il est **t**à	*He is at*

N + vowel make the sound **N**:

Mon avis	Mon **n**avis	*My opinion*
Ton état	Ton **n**état	*Your state*
Son orange	Son **n**orange	*His / Her orange*

F + vowel make the sound **V**:

Neuf ans	Neu **v**ans	*Nine years*

Q + vowel make the sound **K**:

Cinq ans	Cin **k**ans	*Five years*

R + vowel make the sound **R**:

Premier enfant	Premié **r**enfant	*First child*

LINK OR NO LINK?

LINKS ARE REQUIRED BETWEEN or AFTER:

Articles and nouns: Les amis	Les **z**amis	*Friends*
Numbers and nouns: Trois éléphants	Troi **z**éléphants	*Three elephants*
Adjectives and nouns: Bon anniversaire	Bon **n**anniversaire	*Happy birthday*
Pronouns and pronouns: Nous y allons	Nou **zy** allons	*We are going*
Pronouns and verbs: Nous étions	Nou **z**étions	*We were*
After short adverbs: Bien arrivé	Bien **n**arrivé	*Arrived safely*
Chez eux	Chez **z**eux	*At theirs*
Très abordale	Trè **z**abordable	*Very affordable*
Quand est-ce que ... ?	Quan **t**est-ce que ... ?	*When ...?*
Comment allez-vous ?	Commen **t**allez-vous ?	*How are you?*

LINKS ARE OPTIONAL BETWEEN or AFTER:

After long adverbs: Tellement à voir	Tellemen **t**à voir	*So much to see*
Between 2 verbs: Ils sont allés	Ils son **t**allés	*They went*
After plural nouns: Les enfants iront	Les **z**enfants **z**iront	*The children will go*
After "est" and "sont": Il est à l'heure	Il est **t**à l'heure	*He is on time*
Ils sont à l'heure	Ils son **t**à l'heure	*They are in time*

LINKS ARE FORBIDDEN BETWEEN or AFTER:

Before H aspiré: Un haricot	*A bean*
Before 11: Les onze livres	*The eleven books*
Before Oui: C'est oui	*It's yes*
After a name: Douglas a ...	*Douglas has ...*
After a singular noun: Un écran orange	*An orange screen*
After et: Et aussi	*And also*
After comment: Comment as-tu ... ?	*How do you ... ?*
After combien: Combien as-tu ?	*How much do you have?*
After toujours: J'ai toujours eu ...	*I always had ...*
After quand: Quand as-tu ... ?	*When do you have ...?*

**Except for "Comment allez-vous?" and "Quand est-ce que ... ?"*

THE SOUND É [e]

Tongue: Bottom of the mouth
The air goes through: The mouth
Lips: Slightly stretched horizontally

There are **6 different ways** to obtain the sound **É**
4 common ways: **É – AI – ER – EZ**
And 2 less common: **ED - E**

É

Anywhere in the word:

Une **é**cole	*A school*	Un **é**cran	*A screen*
Un d**é**	*A dice*	Une cam**é**ra	*A camera*
Une t**él**évision	*A television*	Un t**él**éphone	*A phone*

At the end of the participle passé of ER verbs:

Mang**é**	*Eaten*
Cherch**é**	*Searched*
All**é**	*Gone*

AI

In specific words:

J'ai	*I have*
Aimer	*To like / To love*

Future forms of verbs with JE:

Je fer**ai**	*I will do / make*
Je manger**ai**	*I will eat*
Je ser**ai**	*I will be*

ER

At the end of nouns:

Un déjeun**er**	*A breakfast*	De l'aci**er**	*Some steel*
Un escali**er**	*A staircase*	Un dang**er**	*A danger*
Un clavi**er**	*A keyboard*	Un casi**er**	*A locker*

THE SOUND É [e]

ER

Informative forms of ER verbs:

Mang**er**	*To eat*
Chant**er**	*To sing*
Regard**er**	*To look / To watch*

EZ

At the end of some words:

Ass**ez**	*Enough*
Un n**ez**	*A nose*
Ch**ez**	*At*

Present forms of verbs with VOUS:

Vous all**ez**	*You go*
Vous cherch**ez**	*You search*
Vous buv**ez**	*You drink*

ED

Un pi**ed**	*A foot*

E

Effacer	*To erase / To delete*

THE WORD “ET”

Et	*And*

THE SOUND É [e]

Listening 2: Focus on É

Bé - Cé - Dé - Fé - Gé - Lé - Mé - Né - Pé - Ré - Sé - Té - Vé - Xé - Zé - Ché - lé

Listening 3: É in words

Bé	Un **bébé**	*A baby*	
Cé	Une **cé**dille	*A cedilla*	
Dé	**Dé**cembre	*December*	
Fé	**Fé**vrier	*February*	
Gé	Chan**gé**	*Changed*	
Lé	**Lé**ger	*Light*	
Mé	**Mé**langé	*Mixed*	
Né	Me**né**	*Led*	
Pé	Une é**pé**e	*A sword*	
Ré	**Ré**pondre	*To answer*	
Sé	Ver**sé**	*Poured*	
Té	Chan**té**	*Sang*	
Vé	La**vé**	*Washed*	
Xé	Ve**xé**	*Upset*	
Zé	**Zé**ro	*Zero*	
Ché	**Ché**ri	*Darling*	
lé	P**lié**	*Folded*	

Listening 4: ER in words

Ber	Tom**ber**	*To fall*	
Cer	Lan**cer**	*To throw*	
Der	Cé**der**	*To transfer*	
Fer	Sur**fer**	*To surf*	
Ger	Un boulan**ger**	*A baker*	
Ler	Pe**ler**	*To peel*	
Mer	Ra**mer**	*To paddle*	
Ner	Le dî**ner**	*The dinner*	
Per	Ta**per**	*To beat*	
Rer	Ga**rer**	*To park*	
Ser	Pen**ser**	*To think*	
Ter	Sau**ter**	*To jump*	
Ver	Le**ver**	*To get up*	
Xer	Ta**xer**	*To tax*	
Zer	Bron**zer**	*To tan*	
Cher	Cher**cher**	*To search*	
ler	Un cla**vier**	*A keyboard*	

THE SOUND É [e]

Listening 5: EZ at the end of words

Bez	Vous go**bez**	*You swallow*	______
Cez	Vous tra**cez**	*You trace*	______
Dez	Vous atten**dez**	*You wait*	______
Fez	Vous sur**fez**	*You surf*	______
Gez	Vous allon**gez**	*You lay down*	______
Lez	Vous al**lez**	*You go*	______
Mez	Vous mi**mez**	*You mimic*	______
Nez	Le **nez**	*The nose*	______
Pez	Vous pom**pez**	*You pump*	______
Rez	Vous ju**rez**	*You swear*	______
Sez	As**sez**	*Enough*	______
Tez	Vous no**tez**	*You note*	______
Vez	Vous rê**vez**	*You dream*	______
Xez	Vous ve**xez**	*You upset*	______
Zez	Vous mi**sez**	*You bet*	______
Chez	**Chez**	*At*	______
Iez	Vous ser**iez**	*You would be*	______

Listening 6: AI at the end of verbs conjugated in "futur simple" with JE

J'aur**ai**	*I will have*	______
Je manger**ai**	*I will eat*	______
Je ser**ai**	*I will be*	______
Je laver**ai**	*I will wash*	______
J'écrir**ai**	*I will write*	______
Je ranger**ai**	*I will tidy*	______
Je prendr**ai**	*I will take*	______
J'étudier**ai**	*I will study*	______
Je rempli**rai**	*I will fill up*	______
Je dormi**rai**	*I will sleep*	______

THE SOUND È [ɛ]

Tongue: Bottom of the mouth
The air goes through: The mouth
Lips: Naturally open

There are **13 different ways** to obtain the sound **È**, some of them including silent letters but I find it important to add them.
11 common ways: **È - Ê - Ë - E - AIS - AIT - AIENT - EI - ET - AI - ES / EST**
And 2 less common: **EY - ECT**

È

Anywhere in the word:

Le p**è**re	*The father*	Une bi**è**re	*A beer*
La m**è**re	*The mother*	La fi**è**vre	*The fever*
Ch**è**re	*Dear (f)*	Fi**è**re	*Proud (f)*

Ê

Anywhere in the word:

Une f**ê**te	*A party*	Un r**ê**ve	*A dream*
Une t**ê**te	*A head*	Une p**ê**che	*A peach*
Une fen**ê**tre	*A window*	La for**ê**t	*The forest*

Ë

No**ë**l	*Christmas*

E

Before the last audible letter:

La m**e**r	*The sea*	Z**e**n	*Zen*
Ch**e**r	*Dear (m)*	N**e**t	*Net*
S**e**c	*Dry*	C**e**t	*This / That*

Before two consonants:

C**e**lle	*This one*	Le r**e**ste	*The rest*
La T**e**rre	*The Earth*	Un v**e**rbe	*A verb*
Une s**e**lle	*A saddle*	Une v**e**ste	*A jacket*

THE SOUND È [ɛ]

AIS

At the end of some words:

Fr**ais**	*Fresh*	M**ais**	*But*
Un Franç**ais**	*A French man*	Un pal**ais**	*A palace*
Jam**ais**	*Never*	Mauv**ais**	*Bad*

Imparfait form of verbs with JE and TU:

Je cherch**ais**	*I looked for / searched*
Tu all**ais**	*You went*
Tu dorm**ais**	*You slept*

Conditionnel form of verbs with JE and TU:

Je chercher**ais**	*I would look for / search*
Tu ir**ais**	*You would go*
Tu dormir**ais**	*You would sleep*

AIT

At the end of some words:

Du l**ait**	*Some milk*	Un extr**ait**	*An extract*
Un f**ait**	*A fact*	Un portr**ait**	*A picture*
Un souh**ait**	*A wish*	Distr**ait**	*Forgetful*

Imparfait form of verbs with IL, ELLE and ON:

Il cherch**ait**	*He looked for / searched*
Elle all**ait**	*She went*
On dorm**ait**	*We slept*

Conditionnel form of verbs with IL, ELLE and ON:

Il chercher**ait**	*He would look for / search*
Elle ir**ait**	*She would go*
On achèter**ait**	*We would buy*

THE SOUND È [ɛ]

AIENT

Imparfait form of verbs with ILS and ELLES:

Ils ét**aient**	*They were*
Elles nage**aient**	*They swam*
Ils cuisin**aient**	*They cooked*

Conditionnel form of verbs with ILS and ELLES:

Ils ser**aient**	*They would be*
Elles nager**aient**	*They would swim*
Ils cuisiner**aient**	*They would cook*

EI

Anywhere in the word:

Une r**ei**ne	*A queen*	Une bal**ei**ne	*A whale*
La n**ei**ge	*The snow*	B**ei**ge	*Beige*
S**ei**ze	*Sixteen*	Une v**ei**ne	*A vein*

ET

At the end of some words:

Un brace**let**	*A bracelet*	Un livr**et**	*A booklet*
Un alphab**et**	*An alphabet*	Mu**et**	*Silent*
Un tabour**et**	*A stool*	Un lac**et**	*A shoelace*

AI

Inside the word:

La l**ai**ne	*The wool*	Cl**ai**r	*Clear*
F**ai**re	*To do / To make*	F**ai**ble	*Weak*
Une fr**ai**se	*A strawberry*	Une ch**ai**se	*A chair*

At the end of some words:

Un bal**ai**	*A broom*
Vr**ai**	*True*
Un dél**ai**	*A deadline*

THE SOUND È [ɛ]

ES - EST

Present form of ÊTRE with TU – IL – ELLE – ON:

Tu **es**	*You are*	Elle **est**	*She is*
Il **est**	*He is*	On **est**	*We are*

ES

In small words such as:

D**es**	*Some*	M**es**	*My*
L**es**	*The*	T**es**	*Your*
C**es**	*These / Those*	S**es**	*His / Her / Its*

**ES can also be pronounced as É*

EY

Un pon**ey**	*A pony*

ECT

Un susp**ect**	*A suspect*
Le resp**ect**	*The respect*
Un asp**ect**	*An aspect*

THE SOUND È [ɛ]

Listening 7: Focus on È

Bè - Cè - Dè - Fè - Gè - Lè - Mè - Nè - Pè - Rè - Sè - Tè - Vè - Xè - Chè - Iè

Listening 8: È in words

Il gèle	*It's freezing*	______________
Une lèvre	*A lip*	______________
La mère	*The mother*	______________
Très	*Very*	______________
Sèche	*Dry (f)*	______________
Chère	*Dear (f)*	______________
Le père	*The father*	______________
Une bière	*A beer*	______________
La fièvre	*The fever*	______________
Fière	*Proud (f)*	______________

Listening 9: Ê in words

Une bête	*A beast*	______________
Une fête	*A party*	______________
Même	*Even*	______________
Une fenêtre	*A window*	______________
Pêcher	*To fish*	______________
Prêter	*To lend*	______________
Une tête	*A head*	______________
Un rêve	*A dream*	______________
Une pêche	*A peach*	______________
La forêt	*The forest*	______________

Listening 10: E before 2 consonants

Celle	*This one*	______________
Une dette	*A debt*	______________
La lecture	*The reading*	______________
Une pelle	*A shovel*	______________
La Terre	*The Earth*	______________
Une selle	*A saddle*	______________
Le reste	*The rest*	______________
Un verbe	*A verb*	______________
Une veste	*A jacket*	______________

THE SOUND È [ɛ]

Listening 11: E before the last audible letter of the word

Avec	*With*	______________
Le g**e**l	*The frost*	______________
La m**e**r	*The sea*	______________
Ch**e**r	*Dear*	______________
S**e**c	*Dry*	______________
Z**e**n	*Zen*	______________
N**e**t	*Net*	______________
C**e**t	*This / That*	______________
T**e**l	*As*	______________

Listening 12: AIS at the end of words

Fr**ais**	*Fresh*	______________
M**ais**	*But*	______________
Un pal**ais**	*A palace*	______________
Un Angl**ais**	*An English man*	______________
Un Franç**ais**	*A French man*	______________
Jam**ais**	*Never*	______________
Un rab**ais**	*A discount*	______________
Mauv**ais**	*Bad*	______________
Ép**ais**	*Thick*	______________
Un harn**ais**	*A harness*	______________

Listening 13: AIT at the end of words

Le l**ait**	*This milk*	______________
Parf**ait**	*Perfect*	______________
Un f**ait**	*A fact*	______________
Un extr**ait**	*An extract*	______________
Un souh**ait**	*A wish*	______________
Satisf**ait**	*Satisfied*	______________
Un portr**ait**	*A picture*	______________
Distr**ait**	*A withdrawal*	______________
Abstr**ait**	*Abstract*	______________

THE SOUND È [ɛ]

Listening 14: EI in words

La r**ei**ne	*The queen*	______
La p**ei**ne	*The sorrow*	______
La n**ei**ge	*The snow*	______
Tr**ei**ze	*Thirteen*	______
S**ei**ze	*Sixteen*	______
B**ei**ge	*Beige*	______
Une bal**ei**ne	*A whale*	______
Une v**ei**ne	*A vein*	______
Fr**ei**ner	*To brake*	______
Le s**ei**gle	*The rye*	______

Listening 15: ET at the end of words

Un bracel**et**	*A bracelet*	______
Un j**et**	*A jet*	______
Un secr**et**	*A secret*	______
Un gil**et**	*A cardigan*	______
Un alphab**et**	*An alphabet*	______
Un tabour**et**	*A stool*	______
Un nav**et**	*A turnip*	______
Un lac**et**	*A shoelace*	______
Un poul**et**	*A chicken*	______
Un obj**et**	*An object*	______

Listening 16: AI at the end of words

La l**ai**ne	*The wool*	______
Un bal**ai**	*A broom*	______
Le dél**ai**	*The time limit*	______
Vr**ai**	*True*	______
F**ai**re	*To do / To make*	______
J'**ai**me	*I like / I love*	______
Une sem**ai**ne	*A week*	______
Une fr**ai**se	*A strawberry*	______
Une **ai**le	*A wing*	______
Une p**ai**re	*A pair*	______

THE SOUND È [ɛ]

Listening 17: AIS – AIT – AIENT at the end of verbs conjugated in "imparfait" or "conditionnel"

Çais – Çait – Çaient	Je lan**çais**	Il lan**çait**	Ils lan**çaient**	*Threw*
Dais – Dait – Daient	Tu cé**dais**	Elle cé**dait**	Elles cé**daient**	*Gave in*
Fais – Fait – Faient	Je sur**fais**	On sur**fait**	Ils sur**faient**	*Surfed*
Geais – Geait – Geaient	Tu man**geais**	Il man**geait**	Elles man**geaient**	*Ate*
Lais – Lait – Laient	J'al**lais**	Elle al**lait**	Ils al**laient**	*Went*
Mais – Mait – Maient	Tu ra**mais**	On ra**mait**	Elles ra**maient**	*Paddled*
Nais – Nait – Naient	Je me**nais**	Elle me**nait**	Ils me**naient**	*Led*
Pais – Pait – Paient	Tu râ**pais**	Il râ**pait**	Elles râ**paient**	*Shredded*
Rais – Rait – Raient	Je di**rais**	On di**rait**	Ils di**raient**	*Would say*
Sais – Sait – Saient	Tu pas**sais**	Il pas**sait**	Elles pas**saient**	*Passed by*
Tais – Tait – Taient	Je chan**tais**	Elle chan**tait**	Ils chan**taient**	*Sang*
Vais – Vait – Vaient	Tu a**vais**	On a**vait**	Elles a**vaient**	*Had*
Xais – Xait – Xaient	Je ve**xais**	Il ve**xait**	Ils ve**xaient**	*Upseted*
Zais – Zait – Zaient	Tu bron**zais**	Elle bron**zait**	Elles bron**zaient**	*Tanned*
Chais – Chait – Chaient	Je cher**chais**	On cher**chait**	Ils cher**chaient**	*Searched*
Iais – Iait – Iaient	Tu pl**iais**	Il pl**iait**	Elles pl**iaient**	*Folded*

Çais – Çait – Çaient	______	______	______
Dais – Dait – Daient	______	______	______
Fais – Fait – Faient	______	______	______
Geais – Geait – Geaient	______	______	______
Lais – Lait – Laient	______	______	______
Mais – Mait – Maient	______	______	______
Nais – Nait – Naient	______	______	______
Pais – Pait – Paient	______	______	______
Rais – Rait – Raient	______	______	______
Sais – Sait – Saient	______	______	______
Tais – Tait – Taient	______	______	______
Vais – Vait – Vaient	______	______	______
Xais – Xait – Xaient	______	______	______
Zais – Zait – Zaient	______	______	______
Chais – Chait – Chaient	______	______	______
Iais – Iait – Iaient	______	______	______

NASAL VOWELS

Try to pronounce the sound **mmmm** while keeping your mouth closed. Then try to pinch your nose – What happens? The sound is impossible to make if you block your nose.

Now try to open your mouth and mmm again. Notice that the air goes through your nose and your mouth.

You just made a **nasal vowel!**

A good example of nasal vowels are the English words

SING – SANG – SUNG - SONG

There are 2 different possibilities for nasal vowels in a word:

Before a consonant, or as the last sound of the word.
Before an oral vowel, it changes the sound completely.
We will see that on the lesson **"Nasal vowels before an oral vowel".**

ON - OM

AN – AM – EN - EM

IN – IM – AIN – AIM – EIN – YN - YM

UN - UM

IEN

OIN

NASAL VOWEL: ON [ɔ̃]

Tongue: Bottom of the mouth
The air goes through: The mouth and the nose
Lips: Rounded

Round you mouth a little and try the **mmm** again, you will pronounce the sound **ON**.

ON

N**on**	*No*
Une chans**on**	*A song*
Une mais**on**	*A house*
Un b**on**b**on**	*A candy*
Un d**on**	*A gift*
L**on**g	*Long*
Un r**on**d	*A round*
S**on**	*His / Her / Its*
M**on**	*My*
T**on**	*Your*

OM Before **B** or **P**

C**om**pter	*To count*
Un n**om**	*A name*
Un z**om**bie	*A zombie*
Un tr**om**bone	*A trombone*
Un p**om**pier	*A firefighter*
Une t**om**be	*A grave*
Un n**om**bre	*A number*

NASAL VOWEL: ON [ɔ̃]

Listening 18: Focus on ON

Bon - Con - Don - Fon - Gon - Jon - Lon - Mon - Non - Pon - Ron - Son - Ton - Von - Zon

Listening 19: ON in words

Bon	**Bon**dé	*Crowded*	__________
Con	**Con**quérir	*To conquer*	__________
Don	Un **don**	*A gift*	__________
Fon	**Fon**der	*To found*	__________
Gon	Une **gon**dole	*A gondola*	__________
Jon	Une **jon**quille	*A daffodil*	__________
Lon	**Lon**gue	*Long (f)*	__________
Mon	**Mon**ter	*To go up*	__________
Non	Un ca**non**	*A cannon*	__________
Pon	Un **pon**t	*A bridge*	__________
Ron	Un bibe**ron**	*A baby bottle*	__________
Son	**Son**ger	*To think*	__________
Ton	Un **tonton**	*An uncle*	__________
Von	Nous bra**von**s	*We brave*	__________
Zon	Nous bron**zon**s	*We tan*	__________

Listening 20: OM in words

C**om**pter	*To count*	__________
R**om**pre	*To break up*	__________
Un c**om**pagnon	*A companion*	__________
Un p**om**pier	*A firefighter*	__________
T**om**ber	*To fall*	__________
Un z**om**bie	*A zombie*	__________
S**om**bre	*Dark*	__________
Une b**om**be	*A bomb*	__________
Les c**om**bles	*The attic*	__________
L**om**baire	*Lumbar*	__________
Un n**om**	*A name*	__________
Un tr**om**bone	*A trombone*	__________

NASAL VOWEL: AN [ɑ̃]

Tongue: Bottom of the mouth
The air goes through: The mouth and the nose
Lips: Between rounded and naturally open

The sound AN has 4 different spellings: **AN – AM** and **EN – EM**
Place your lips like you are about to pronounce the letter A and make a nasal sound.

AN

Le s**ang**	*The blood*
T**an**t	*So much*
Ch**an**ger	*To change*
Un **an**	*A year*
Un éléph**ant**	*An elephant*
Un **an**ge	*An angel*
Une **an**cre	*An anchor*
Une ch**an**son	*A song*
Mam**an**	*Mom*
Un b**an**c	*A bench*

AM Before **B** or **P**

Un ch**am**p	*A field*
Un ch**am**pignon	*A mushroom*
Un j**am**bon	*A ham*
Un t**am**bour	*A drum*
Une **am**bulance	*An ambulance*
Une **am**poule	*A lightbulb*
Une j**am**be	*A leg*
Un t**am**pon	*A tampon*
Une r**am**pe	*A ramp*
Un b**am**bou	*A bamboo*

EN

L**en**t	*Slow*
Les **en**fants	*The children*
Le v**en**tre	*The stomach*
V**en**dredi	*Friday*
Une d**en**t	*A tooth*
Le v**en**t	*The wind*
Entourer	*To circle*
Une **en**veloppe	*An envelope*
Le c**en**tre	*The center*
Cont**en**t	*Happy*

EM Before **B** or **P**

Le t**em**ps	*The weather*
La t**em**pérature	*The temperature*
R**em**plir	*To fill up*
Nov**em**bre	*November*
Déc**em**bre	*December*
Embrasser	*To kiss*
Une t**em**pête	*A storm*
S**em**bler	*To seem*
Le print**em**ps	*Spring*
Ens**em**ble	*Together*

AON pronounced AN (Irregular)

Un f**aon**	*A fawn*
Un t**aon**	*A horsefly*
Un p**aon**	*A peacock*

NASAL VOWEL: AN [ɑ̃]

Listening 21: Focus on AN

Ban - Can - Dan - Fan - Gan - Jan - Lan - Man - Pan - Ran - San - Tan - Van - Chan

Listening 22: AN in words

Ban	La b**an**c	*The bench*	______
Can	La c**an**tine	*The cantina*	______
Dan	D**an**s	*In*	______
Fan	Un f**an**tôme	*A ghost*	______
Gan	Un g**an**t	*A glove*	______
Jan	J**an**vier	*January*	______
Lan	Un gl**an**d	*An acorn*	______
Man	M**an**quer	*To miss*	______
Pan	Un p**an**talon	*A pants*	______
Ran	Une r**an**çon	*A ransom*	______
San	Le s**an**g	*The blood*	______
Tan	T**an**t	*So much*	______
Van	V**an**ter	*To brag*	______
Chan	Ch**an**ger	*To change*	______

Listening 23: AM in words

Un b**am**bou	*A bamboo*	______
C**am**per	*To camp*	______
Une j**am**be	*A leg*	______
Un p**am**plemousse	*A grapefruit*	______
R**am**per	*To crawl*	______
Un v**am**pire	*A vampire*	______
Un ch**am**pignon	*A mushroom*	______
Un ch**am**p	*A field*	______
Un j**am**bon	*A ham*	______
Une **am**bulance	*An ambulance*	______
Un t**am**pon	*A tampon*	______
Une r**am**pe	*A ramp*	______
Un ch**am**pion	*A champion*	______
Une l**am**pe	*A lamp*	______

NASAL VOWEL: AN [ã]

Listening 24: EN in words

C**en**t	*Hundred*	________
Une d**en**t	*A tooth*	________
Des g**en**s	*Some people*	________
L**en**t	*Slow*	________
M**en**tir	*To lie*	________
P**en**dant	*During*	________
Pr**en**dre	*To take*	________
S**en**tir	*To smell / To feel*	________
T**en**ter	*To try*	________
Le v**en**t	*The wind*	________

Listening 25: EM in words

Déc**em**bre	*December*	________
Nov**em**bre	*November*	________
R**em**plir	*To fill up*	________
Le t**em**ps	*The weather*	________
Emboîter	*To slot*	________
Embuer	*To fog up*	________
Un **em**bout	*A nozzle*	________
Empirer	*To worsen*	________
Emparer	*To grab*	________
Embêter	*To annoy*	________

NASAL VOWEL: IN [ɛ̃]

Tongue: Bottom of the mouth
The air goes through: The mouth and the nose
Lips: Slightly stretched horizontally

The sound IN has 7 different spellings: **IN – IM – AIN – EIN – AIM – YN – YM.**
Stretch your mouth horizontally like you are about to make the **sound I** and add the nasal sound.

IN

Le jard**in**	*The yard*
Le s**in**ge	*The monkey*
Le lap**in**	*The rabbit*
Le pouss**in**	*The chick*
La f**in**	*The end*
Af**in**	*Therefore*
Un chem**in**	*A path*
C**in**q	*Five*
Un cous**in**	*A cousin*
Un c**in**tre	*A hanger*

IM Before **B** or **P**

S**im**ple	*Simple*
Impossible	*Impossible*
Le t**im**bre	*The stamp*
Gr**im**per	*To climb*
Une **im**passe	*An impasse*
Imposer	*To impose*
Un **im**pact	*An impact*
Un **im**posteur	*An impostor*
Un l**im**be	*A limb*
Un **im**pôt	*A tax*

AIN

Un p**ain**	*A bread*
Une m**ain**	*A hand*
Dem**ain**	*Tomorrow*
Un b**ain**	*A bath*
Vil**ain**	*Ugly*
Urb**ain**	*Urban*
Un hum**ain**	*A human*
Un gr**ain**	*A grain*
Un cop**ain**	*A friend*
Un tr**ain**	*A train*

EIN

Une p**ein**ture	*A painting*
Un fr**ein**	*A brake*
Une c**ein**ture	*A belt*
Un s**ein**	*A breast*
Un r**ein**	*A kidney*
Ét**ein**dre	*To turn off*
P**ein**dre	*To paint*
Une t**ein**ture	*A dye*
Att**ein**dre	*To reach*
Pl**ein**	*Full*

NASAL VOWEL: IN [ɛ̃]

AIM

La **faim**	*The hunger*
Un d**aim**	*A deer*
Un ess**aim**	*A swarm*

YN

Un l**yn**x	*A lynx*
Un lar**yn**x	*A larynx*

YM

Le th**ym**	*The thyme*
S**ym**pa	*Nice*
Le t**ym**pan	*The eardrum*
Un s**ym**bole	*A symbol*

EN (IRREGULAR)

Un exam**en**	*An exam*

NASAL VOWEL: IN [ɛ̃]

Listening 26: Focus on IN

Bin - Cin - Din - Fin - Gin - Jin - Lin - Min - Pin - Rin - Sin - Tin - Vin - Chin

Listening 27: IN in words

Le jard**in**	*The yard*	
La f**in**	*The end*	
Le lap**in**	*The rabbit*	
Un br**in**	*A strand*	
Le s**in**ge	*The monkey*	
Un **in**stant	*An instant*	
Un pouss**in**	*A chick*	
Un couss**in**	*A cushion*	
Un bass**in**	*A basin*	
Un c**in**tre	*A hanger*	

Listening 28: IM in words

Gr**im**per	*To climb*	
S**im**ple	*Simple*	
Un t**im**bre	*A stamp*	
Impossible	*Impossible*	
Du den**im**	*Denim*	
Impur	*Impure*	
Impair	*Odd*	
Impayé	*Unpaid*	
Impoli	*Rude*	
Un **im**pact	*An impact*	

NASAL VOWEL: IN [ɛ̃]

Listening 29: AIN in words

Un b**ain**	*A bath*	______
Dem**ain**	*Tomorrow*	______
Un p**ain**	*A bread loaf*	______
Un s**ain**t	*A saint*	______
V**ain**	*Vain*	______
Une m**ain**	*A hand*	______
Un n**ain**	*A dwarf*	______
Un g**ain**	*A gain*	______
Un dr**ain**	*A drain*	______
Ainsi	*Thus*	______

Listening 30: EIN in words

Une c**ein**ture	*A belt*	______
Pl**ein**	*Full*	______
Une p**ein**ture	*A painting*	______
Un s**ein**	*A breast*	______
Un fr**ein**	*A brake*	______
Le t**ein**t	*The complexion*	______
Une t**ein**ture	*A dye*	______
Un r**ein**	*A kidney*	______
Ét**ein**dre	*To turn off*	______

NASAL VOWEL: UN [œ̃]

Tongue: Bottom of the mouth
The air goes through: The mouth and the nose
Lips: Between rounded and naturally open

UN is pronounced the same way as **IN – IM – AIN – EIN – AIM – YN – YM** in Northern France and Belgium, including Paris.
The pronunciation as **[œ̃]** is lower than the sound IN. It's a mix between **E** and **IN**.

UN

Chac**un**	*Each*
Br**un**	*Brown*
Un	*A*
L**un**di	*Monday*
Empr**un**ter	*To borrow*
Auc**un**	*None*
La j**un**gle	*The jungle*
Comm**un**	*Common*

UM

H**um**ble	*Humble*
Le parf**um**	*The perfume*

Listening 31: UN in words

Chac**un**	*Each*	______
Br**un**	*Brown*	______
Un	*A*	______
L**un**di	*Monday*	______
Empr**un**ter	*To borrow*	______
Auc**un**	*None*	______
La j**un**gle	*The jungle*	______
Comm**un**	*Common*	______

Listening 32: UM in words

H**um**ble	*Humble*	______
Le parf**um**	*The perfume*	______

IEN [jɛ̃]

Tongue: The bottom / The middle of the tongue touches the palate
The air goes through: The mouth and the nose
Lips: Slightly stretched horizontally

We could think that **IEN** would be pronounced I followed by the sound **EN** but it's pronounced slightly differently.
The pronunciation is as followed: **I – IN = [jɛ̃]**

IEN

Un b**ien**	*A property*
Un music**ien**	*A musician*
Un ch**ien**	*A dog*
M**ien**	*Mine*
T**ien**	*Yours*
R**ien**	*Nothing*
Un gard**ien**	*A guardian*
Un coméd**ien**	*A comedian*
Un l**ien**	*A link*
B**ien**tôt	*Soon*

Listening 33: Focus on IEN
Bien - Cien - Dien - Lien - Mien - Sien - Tien - Vien - Chien

Listening 34: IEN in words

Bien	Un b**ien**	*A property*	______
Cien	Un music**ien**	*A musician*	______
Dien	Un gard**ien**	*A guardian*	______
Lien	Un l**ien**	*A link*	______
Mien	M**ien**	*Mine*	______
Sien	**Sien**	*His / Hers*	______
Tien	**Tien**	*Yours*	______
Vien	V**ien**s	*Come*	______
Chien	Un ch**ien**	*A dog*	______

OIN [wɛ̃]

Tongue: Bottom of the mouth
The air goes through: The mouth and the nose
Lips: From rounded to slightly stretched horizontally

The equivalent of: **W – IN = [wɛ̃]**

OIN

M**oin**s	*Less*
Un s**oin**	*A care*
L**oin**	*Far*
Rej**oin**dre	*To join*
Un j**oin**t	*A joint*
Un c**oin**	*A corner*
Une p**oin**te	*A tip*
Du f**oin**	*Some hay*
Un shamp**oin**g	*A shampoo*
Un bes**oin**	*A need*

Listening 35: OIN in words

M**oin**s	*Less*	__________
Un s**oin**	*A care*	__________
L**oin**	*Far*	__________
Rej**oin**dre	*To join*	__________
Un j**oin**t	*A joint*	__________
Un c**oin**	*A corner*	__________
Une p**oin**te	*A tip*	__________
Du f**oin**	*Some hay*	__________
Un shamp**oin**g	*A shampoo*	__________
Un bes**oin**	*A need*	__________

VOWEL AFTER A NASAL VOWEL

When a nasal vowel is followed by an oral vowel, you have to pronounce every letter of it. For example:

UN and UM

Le parf**um**	Parfumer	*The perfume*	*To perfume*
Un	Une	*A (m)*	*A (f)*
Br**un**	Brune	*Brown (m)*	*Brown (f)*
Chac**un**	Chacune	*Each (m)*	*Each (f)*

IN, EIN and AIN

Un jard**in**	Jardiner	*A garden*	*To garden*
F**in**	Fine	*Thin (m)*	*Thin (f)*
Un fr**ein**	Freiner	*A brake*	*To brake*
Cert**ain**	Certaine	*Certain (m)*	*Certain (f)*

DOUBLE N

B**on**	Bonne	*Good (m)*	*Good (f)*
Un d**on**	Donner	*A gift*	*To give*
M**ien**	Mienne	*Mine (m)*	*Mine (f)*
T**ien**	Tienne	*Yours (m)*	*Yours (f)*
S**ien**	Sienne	*His / Hers (m)*	*His / Hers (f)*
Un ch**ien**	Une chienne	*A dog (m)*	*A dog (f)*

DOUBLE M

Un n**om**	Nommer	*A name*	*To name*

VOWELS AND VOWEL SOUNDS

A

E

EU - ŒU

I - Y

OPEN O – CLOSE O **O – Ô – EAU - AU**

OI

U - OU

UI

IL - ILLE

AIL - AILLE

EIL – EILLE – AYE

OUILLE

ŒIL – EUIL – EUILLE – UEIL

A [a] – [ɑ]

Tongue: Bottom of the mouth
The air goes through: The mouth
Lips: Naturally open

A _ _ _ _	**A**	[a]	Un **a**chat *A purchase*	**A**voir *To have*	**A**ller *To go*
_ _ **a** _ _	**A**	[a]	P**a**r *By*	Une m**a**rre *A pond*	Une t**a**sse *A cup*
_ _ _ _ **a**	**A**	[a]	S**a** *His / Her / Its*	Fer**a** *Will do*	Ir**a** *Will go*
À	**A**	[a]	L**à** *There*	Voil**à** *Here*	Déj**à** *Already*
Â	**A**	[ɑ]	Une t**â**che *A task*	Un l**â**che *A coward*	Avoir h**â**te *Can't wait*

Listening 36: Focus on A
Ba – Ca – Da – Fa – Ga – La – Ma – Na – Pa – Ra – Sa – Ta – Va – Za – Cha

Listening 37: A in words

Ba	Une **ba**tte	*A bat*	______________
Ca	Une **ca**ve	*A cave*	______________
Da	Une **da**te	*A date*	______________
Fa	**Fa**de	*Bland*	______________
Ga	Un **gâ**teau	*A cake*	______________
La	Une **la**tte	*A ruler*	______________
Ma	Une **ma**man	*A mother*	______________
Na	Une **na**tte	*A braid*	______________
Pa	Un **papa**	*A dad*	______________
Ra	**Ra**ter	*To fail*	______________
Sa	Un **sa**pin	*A fir tree*	______________
Ta	Une **ta**rte	*A pie*	______________
Va	**Va**rier	*To vary*	______________
Za	Un lé**za**rd	*A lizard*	______________
Cha	**Cha**cun	*Each*	______________

E [ə]

Tongue: Bottom of the mouth
The air goes through: The mouth
Lips: Rounded

_ _ **e** _ _	**E**	**[ə]**	Une c**e**rise *A cherry*	Un ch**e**val *A horse*	Un m**e**lon *A cantaloupe*
_ **e** *2 letters words*	**E**	**[ə]**	J**e** *I*	D**e** *Of / For / By*	L**e** *The*
_ _ **e** *3 letters words*	**E**	**[ə]**	Qu**e** *That*		
_ _ **e** _ _	**/**		Un bib**e**ron *A baby bottle*	Une boulang**e**rie *A bakery*	All**e**magne *Germany*
_ _ _ _ **e**	**/**		Une semain**e** *A week*	Une chemis**e** *A shirt*	Un livr**e** *A book*
_ **ai** _ _ _	**E**	**[ə]**	Je f**ai**sais *I did*	Nous f**ai**sions *We did*	Ils f**ai**saient *They did*
_ **e** _ _ _	**A**	**[a]**	Une f**e**mme *A woman*	Évid**e**mment *Obviously*	Prud**e**mment *Carefully*

**See more examples for E = A and AI = E on "Unusual pronunciation"*

E [ə]

Listening 38: Focus on E

Be – Ce – De – Fe – Ge – Je – Le – Me – Ne – Pe – Re – Se – Te – Ve – Ze – Che

Listening 39: E in words

Be	Une **be**lette	*A weasel*	______
Ce	Une **ce**rise	*A cherry*	______
De	**De**	*Of / For / By*	______
Fe	Une **fe**nêtre	*A window*	______
Ge	Un **ge**nou	*A knee*	______
Je	Un **je**ton	*A token*	______
Le	Un pamp**le**mousse	*A grapefruit*	______
Me	Un **me**lon	*A cantaloupe*	______
Ne	**Ne**	*(part of negation)*	______
Pe	**Pe**tit	*Small*	______
Re	**Re**faire	*To do again*	______
Se	**Se**ra	*Will be*	______
Te	Un dé**te**nu	*An inmate*	______
Ve	**Ve**nir	*To come*	______
Ze	Ra**se**ra	*Will shave*	______
Che	Un **che**val	*A horse*	______

Listening 40: Mute E in words

Un bib**e**ron	*A baby bottle*	______
Une boulang**e**rie	*A bakery*	______
All**e**magne	*Germany*	______
Rapid**e**ment	*Quickly*	______
Lent**e**ment	*Slowly*	______
Un rang**e**ment	*A storage*	______
Un brac**e**let	*A bracelet*	______
Un pass**e**port	*A passport*	______
Une env**e**loppe	*An envelope*	______
Une prom**e**nade	*A walk*	______
Nous nag**e**ons	*We swim*	______

EU - ŒU [ø] – [œ]

Tongue: Bottom of the mouth
The air goes through: The mouth
Lips: Rounded

The letters combination **EU / ŒU** can have two different pronunciations, depending where it's placed in the word. We called the different sounds **"open sound"** and **"close sound".** **"Open sound"** when it's the last sound of the word, and **"close sound"** when a consonant follows and simply closes the sound.

P**eu**x *vs* P**eu**r	*Can vs Fear*
Eux *vs* H**eu**re	*Them vs Hour*
N**œu**d *vs* N**eu**f	*Knot vs Nine*

Listening 41: Open EU – ŒU [ø]

Je p**eu**x	*I can*
Eux	*Them*
Un n**œu**d	*A knot*
D**eu**x	*Two*
Un v**œu**	*A wish*
P**eu**	*Little*
Des chev**eu**x	*Hair*
Le mili**eu**	*The middle*
Un adi**eu**	*A farewell*
Bl**eu**	*Blue*
Un j**eu**	*A game*
Le f**eu**	*The fire*

Listening 42: Close EU – ŒU [œ]

La p**eu**r	*The fear*
Une h**eu**re	*An hour*
N**eu**f	*Nine*
Un **œu**f	*An egg*
S**eu**l	*Alone*
Un c**œu**r	*A heart*
Un tract**eu**r	*A tractor*
Une fl**eu**r	*A flower*
Un doct**eu**r	*A doctor*
Un ordinat**eu**r	*A computer*
Une s**œu**r	*A sister*
Un m**eu**ble	*A piece of furniture*

*See how the different pronunciations impact irregular plurals on "Unusual pronunciation"

I - Y [i] – [j]

Tongue: Middle of the tongue touches the palate
The air goes through: The mouth
Lips: Slightly stretched horizontally

I _ _ _ _	**I**	**[i]**	Une **i**dée *An idea*	**I**vre *Drunk*	**I**ci *Here*
_ _ i _ _	**I**	**[i]**	Un l**i**vre *A book*	Un l**i**t *A bed*	Un k**i**w**i** *A kiwi*
_ _ _ _ i *3 letters words*	**I**	**[i]**	Un**i** *Unified*	Un pl**i** *A fold*	Un tax**i** *A taxi*
î	**I**	**[i]**	Une **î**le *An island*	Un g**î**te *A lodge*	
Ï	**I**	**[i]**	Ana**ï**s	Du ma**ï**s *Some corn*	
y	**I**	**[i]**	Un c**y**cle *A cycle*	Un h**y**mne *An anthem*	
I *Before a vowel*	**Y**	**[j]**	D**i**eu *God*	B**i**en *Good*	S**i**en *His / Hers / Its*
Y _ _ _ _	**Y**	**[j]**	Les **y**eux *The eyes*	Un **y**acht *A yacht*	
Y *Between 2 vowels*	**Y**	**[j]**	Ro**y**al *Royal*	Jo**y**eux *Happy*	

I - Y [i] – [j]

Listening 43: Focus on I

Bi – Ci – Di – Fi – Gi – Hi – Li – Mi – Ni – Pi – Ri – Si – Ti – Vi – Chi

Listening 44: I in words

Bi	Une **bi**beron	*A baby bottle*	________
Ci	Une **ci**tation	*A quote*	________
Di	**Di**re	*To say / To tell*	________
Fi	Un **fi**ls	*A son*	________
Gi	Un **gî**te	*A lodge*	________
Hi	Un **hi**bou	*An owl*	________
Li	Un **li**t	*A bed*	________
Mi	Un **mi**rage	*A mirage*	________
Ni	**Ni**	*Neither*	________
Pi	La **pi**tié	*The pity*	________
Ri	La **ri**vière	*The river*	________
Si	Une **si**rène	*A siren*	________
Ti	**Ti**rer	*To pull*	________
Vi	**Vi**rer	*To fire*	________
Chi	**Chi**caner	*To make a fuss*	________

Listening 45: I [j] in words

Dixième	*Tenth*	________
Un musicien	*A musician*	________
Fier	*Proud*	________
Hier	*Yesterday*	________
Nier	*To deny*	________
Royal	*Royal*	________
Joyeux	*Happy*	________
Mien	*Mine*	________
Tien	*Yours*	________
Un lien	*A link*	________
Un chien	*A dog*	________

O [ɔ] O – Ô – EAU – AU [o]

Tongue: Bottom of the mouth
The air goes through: The mouth
Lips: Rounded

Depending where the letter **O**, or the letters combination **EAU - AU**, are situated, the sound will be an **"open O"** or a **"close O".**
O before a consonant is pronounced as a short **O**, which is the **"close O".**
When **O** is the last sound of the word (or before the sound z), the sound will be longer, called **"open O".**

_ _ **o** _ _	**O**	**[ɔ]**	D**o**ter *To provide*	R**o**ter *To burp*	Fr**o**tter *To rube*
O *as the last sound*	**O**	**[o]**	Un m**o**t *A word*	Un l**o**t *A lot*	Le d**o**s *The back*
Os _	**O**	**[o]**	R**o**se *Pink*	Une p**o**se *A pose*	
Ô	**O**	**[o]**	Un fant**ô**me *A ghost*	**Ô**ter *To remove*	T**ô**t *Early*
AU	**O**	**[o]**	Une p**au**se *A break*	La s**au**ce *The sauce*	**Au**cun *None*
EAU	**O**	**[o]**	Un gât**eau** *A cake*	Un chât**eau** *A castle*	B**eau** *Beautiful*

Listening 46: Close [ɔ] in words

F**o**rt	*Strong*
D**o**nner	*To give*
La m**o**de	*The fashion*
Le s**o**l	*The floor*
Un din**o**saure	*A dinosaur*
Un acc**o**rd	*An agreement*
Al**o**rs	*Then*
Le fr**o**mage	*The cheese*
Le s**o**leil	*The sun*

Listening 47: open [o] in words

Ch**au**d	*Hot*
Un ois**eau**	*A bird*
Un mant**eau**	*A coat*
Autre	*Other*
Une c**ô**te	*A rib*
Un m**o**t	*A word*
Un jum**eau**	*A twin*
F**au**x	*False*
Un rés**eau**	*A network*

OI [wa]

Tongue: Bottom of the mouth
The air goes through: The mouth
Lips: From rounded to slightly stretched horizontally

OI	**wa**	**[wa]**	Le s**oi**r *The evening*	Un ch**oi**x *A choice*	Une **oie** *A goose*

Listening 48: Focus on OI
Boi – Doi – Foi – Joi – Loi – Moi – Noi – Poi – Roi – Soi – Toi – Voi – Choi

Listening 49: OI in words

Boi	**Boi**re	*To drink*	______
Doi	Un **doi**gt	*A finger*	______
Foi	Une **foi**s	*Once*	______
Joi	La **joi**e	*The joy*	______
Loi	La **loi**	*The low*	______
Moi	**Moi**	*Me*	______
Noi	**Noi**r	*Black*	______
Poi	Le **poi**ds	*The weight*	______
Roi	Le **roi**	*The king*	______
Soi	**Soi**	*Self*	______
Toi	**Toi**	*You*	______
Voi	**Voi**r	*To see*	______
Choi	**Choi**sir	*To choose*	______

U [y] OU [u] - [w]

Tongue: Bottom of the mouth
The air goes through: The mouth
Lips: Rounded

U	**u**	**[y]**	Une ch**u**te *A fall*	La l**u**tte *The fight*	Un m**u**rm**u**re *A whisper*
Û	**u**	**[y]**	Une fl**û**te *A flute*	Une b**û**che *A log*	Un b**û**cheron *A lumberjack*
U after G	/		La lang**ue** *The tongue*	Long**ue** *Long (f)*	Une g**u**itare *A guitar*
U after Q	/		Une q**ue**ue *A tail*	Un q**u**art *A quarter*	Q**ue** *That*
OU – OÙ	**ou**	**[u]**	V**ou**s *You*	La s**ou**pe *The soup*	**Où** *Where*
OU *Before a vowel*	**w**	**[w]**	**Ou**i *Yes*	Un j**ou**et *A toy*	L'**ou**est *The west*

Listening 50: Focus on U
Bu – Du – Fu – Ju – Lu – Mu– Nu – Pu – Ru – Su – Tu – Vu – Chu

Listening 51: Focus on OU
Bou – Dou – Fou – Jou – Lou – Mou– Nou – Pou – Rou – Sou – Tou – Vu – Chou

Listening 52 : U and OU in words

Drank	B**u**	La b**ou**e	*The mud*
A bottom	Un c**u**l	Le c**ou**	*The neck*
Some	D**u**	D**ou**x	*Sweet*
I swear	Je j**u**re	Le j**ou**r	*The day*
Some juice	D**u** j**u**s	La j**ou**e	*The cheek*
Read	L**u**	Le l**ou**p	*The wolf*
The sweater	Le p**u**ll	Une p**ou**le	*A chicken*
Pure	P**u**r	P**ou**r	*For*
The street	La r**u**e	La r**ou**e	*The wheel*
On top	Dess**u**s	Dess**ou**s	*Under*
You	T**u**	T**ou**t	*All*
Seen	V**u**	V**ou**s	*You*

UI [ɥ]

Tongue: Middle of the tongue touches the palate
The air goes through: The mouth
Lips: From rounded to slightly stretched horizontally

UI	**wi**	[ɥ]	Une n**ui**t *A night*	F**ui**r *To flee*	L**ui** *Him*

Listening 53: Focus on UI
Bui – Cui – Dui – Fui – Jui – Lui – Nui – Pui – Rui – Sui – Tui

Listening 54: UI in words

Bui	Un **bui**sson	*A bush*	__________
Cui	La **cui**sson	*The cooking*	__________
Dui	En**dui**te	*Coated (f)*	__________
Fui	**Fui**r	*To flee*	__________
Jui	**Jui**llet	*July*	__________
Lui	**Lui**re	*To glow*	__________
Nui	La **nui**t	*The night*	__________
Pui	**Pui**s	*Then*	__________
Rui	Le **rui**sseau	*The stream*	__________
Sui	Je **sui**s	*I am*	__________
Tui	La **tui**le	*The tile*	__________

IL - ILLE [ij] – [il]

Tongue: Middle of the tongue touches the palate
The air goes through: The mouth
Lips: Slightly stretched horizontally

This sound is divided in 2 different sounds, the sound **[i]** followed by the sound **[j]**.

IL - ILLE	**I-Y**	**[ij]**	La fam**ille** *The family*	La van**ille** *The vanilla*	Une chen**ille** *A caterpillar*
ILLE	**IL**	**[il]**	M**ille** *Thousand*	La v**ille** *The city*	Tranqu**ille** *Quiet*

Listening 54: Ul in words

La fam**ille**	*The family*	____________
La van**ille**	*The vanilla*	____________
Une chen**ille**	*A caterpillar*	____________
Gent**il**	*Kind (m)*	____________
Gent**ille**	*Kind (f)*	____________
Une f**ille**	*A girl*	____________
Une qu**ille**	*A bowling pin*	____________
Une gr**ille**	*A grid*	____________
Les pap**ille**s	*The tastebuds*	____________
Un gor**ille**	*A gorilla*	____________

AIL - AILLE [aj]

Tongue: Middle of the tongue touches the palate
The air goes through: The mouth
Lips: From naturally open to slightly stretched horizontally

This sound is divided in 2 different sounds, the sound **[a]** followed by the sound **[j]**.

AIL	**A-Y**	**[aj]**	Un évent**ail** *A fan*	Le trav**ail** *The work*	De l'**ail** *Some garlic*
AILLE	**A-Y**	**[aj]**	Une bat**aille** *A battle*	Trav**aille**r *To work*	Une p**aille** *A straw*

Listening 56: AIL / AILLE in words

Un évent**ail**	*A fan*	____________
Trav**aille**r	*To work*	____________
Une p**aille**	*A straw*	____________
Une m**aille**	*A mesh*	____________
De la vol**aille**	*Some chicken*	____________
Une bat**aille**	*A battle*	____________
Un épouvant**ail**	*A scarecrow*	____________
Une ent**aille**	*A cut*	____________
De l'**ail**	*Some garlic*	____________
Un dét**ail**	*A detail*	____________

EIL - EILLE - AY [ɛj]

Tongue: Middle of the tongue touches the palate
The air goes through: The mouth
Lips: From naturally open to slightly stretched horizontally

This sound is divided in 2 different sounds, the sound **[ɛ]** followed by the sound **[j]**.

EIL	**È-Y**	**[ɛj]**	L'év**eil** *The awaking*	Le sol**eil** *The sun*	Par**eil** *Same*
EILLE	**È-Y**	**[ɛj]**	Une gros**eille** *A redcurrant*	Une bout**eille** *A bottle*	Une merv**eille** *A wonder*
AY	**È-Y**	**[ɛj]**	Ess**ay**er *To try*	**Pay**er *To pay*	**Ray**er *To scratch*

Exception for the word "PAYS" - See "unusual pronunciation"

Listening 57: EIL / EILLE in words

L'év**eil**	*The awakening*	____________
Le sol**eil**	*The sun*	____________
Par**eil**	*Same*	____________
Une gros**eille**	*A redcurrant*	____________
Une bout**eille**	*A bottle*	____________
Une merv**eille**	*A wonder*	____________
Le somm**eil**	*The sleep*	____________
Le rév**eil**	*The alarm clock*	____________
Un cons**eil**	*An advice*	____________
Une or**eille**	*An ear*	____________

Listening 58: AY in words

Ess**ay**er	*To try*	____________
Payer	*To pay*	____________
Rayer	*To scratch*	____________
Ég**ay**er	*To brighten*	____________
Bal**ay**er	*To broom*	____________
Effr**ay**er	*To scare*	____________

OUILLE [uj]

Tongue: Middle of the tongue touches the palate
The air goes through: The mouth
Lips: From naturally open to slightly stretched horizontally

This sound is divided in 2 different sounds, the sound **[u]** followed by the sound **[j]**.

OUILLE	**OU-Y**	**[uj]**	Une gren**ouille** *A frog*	Les n**ouille**s *The noodles*	La f**ouille** *The search*

Listening 59: OUILLE in words

Une **grenouille**	*A frog*	______
Les n**ouille**s	*The noodles*	______
La f**ouille**	*The search*	______
Une ratat**ouille**	*A ratatouille*	______
Une garg**ouille**	*A gargoyle*	______
D**ouille**t	*Cozy*	______
Verr**ouille**r	*To lock*	______
La r**ouille**	*The rust*	______
M**ouille**r	*To wet*	______
Une dép**ouille**	*The remains*	______

ŒIL - EUIL - EUILLE - UEIL [œj]

Tongue: Middle of the tongue touches the palate
The air goes through: The mouth
Lips: From naturally open to slightly stretched horizontally

This sound is divided in 2 different sounds, the sound **[œ]** followed by the sound **[j]**.

After "**C**" and "**G**", it's spelled **UEIL - UEILLE**.

ŒIL	**E-Y**	**[œj]**	Un **œil** *An eye*		
EUIL	**E-Y**	**[œj]**	Le s**euil** *The doorstep*	Le faut**euil** *The armchair*	Une écur**euil** *A squirrel*
EUILLE	**E-Y**	**[œj]**	Une f**euille** *A sheet*	Un portef**euille** *A wallet*	
UEIL	**E-Y**	**[œj]**	L'acc**ueil** *The reception*	Un cerc**ueil** *A coffin*	L'org**ueil** *The pride*

Listening 60: EUIL / EUILLE / UEIL / UEILL in words

Le s**euil**	*The doorstep*	________
Le faut**euil**	*The armchair*	________
Une f**euille**	*A sheet*	________
Un portef**euille**	*A wallet*	________
L'acc**ueil**	*The reception*	________
Acc**ueill**ir	*To welcome*	________
Un cerc**ueil**	*A coffin*	________
L'org**ueil**	*The pride*	________
C**ueill**ir	*To pick*	________

CONSONANTS

B

HARD C - SOFT C

CH

D

F - PH

HARD G - SOFT G

J

H

K - QU

L

M

N - GN

P

R

S - Z

T

V

W

X

B [b]

Tongue: Bottom of the mouth
The air goes through: The mouth
Lips: Close to open – From inside to outside

B _ _ _ _	**B**	**[b]**	**B**eau *Beautiful*	**B**run *Brown*	**B**oire *To drink*
_ _ b _ _	**B**	**[b]**	Un ha**b**it *A piece of clothe*	Un a**b**us *A abuse*	Un ar**b**re *A tree*
_ _ _ _ b	**B**	**[b]**	Le clu**b** *The club*	Le toubi**b** *The doctor*	Sno**b** *Snob*
_ _ _ _ b	**/**		Du plom**b** *Some lead*		
_ _ bs _ _	**PS**	**[ps]**	A**bs**olument *Absolutely*	A**bs**ent *Absent*	

B [b]

Listening 61: Focus on B

Ba – Bé – Bê – Bi – Bo – Bu – Br – Ban – Bon – Bien – Boi – Bou – Beau – Bille – Beille – Bouill

Listening 62: B in words

Ba	**Ba**ttre	*To beat*	______
Bé	Un **bébé**	*A baby*	______
Bê	Une **bê**te	*A beast*	______
Bi	Un **bi**beron	*A baby bottle*	______
Bo	Une **bo**tte	*A boot*	______
Bu	Un a**bu**s	*An abuse*	______
Br	**Br**un	*Brown*	______
Ban	Un a**ban**don	*An abandonment*	______
Bon	La **bon**té	*The goodness*	______
Bien	Un **bien**	*A property*	______
Boi	**Boi**re	*To drink*	______
Bou	Une **bou**teille	*A bottle*	______
Beau	La **beau**té	*The beauty*	______
Bille	Ha**biller**	*To dress up*	______
Beille	Une a**beille**	*A bee*	______
Bouill	**Bouill**ir	*To boil*	______

HARD C [k] SOFT C [s]

HARD C

Tongue: Middle of the tongue touches the palate
The air goes through: The mouth
Lips: Slightly rounded

SOFT C

Tongue: Tip touches the palate, not the teeth
The air goes through: The mouth
Lips: Slightly stretched horizontally

C + a.o.u	**K**	**[k]**	**C**ontre *Against*	**C**arré *Square*	La **c**ulture *The culture*
_ **cc** _ _	**K**	**[k]**	O**cc**uper *To occupy*	A**cc**user *To accuse*	Un a**cc**ord *An agreement*
_ _ _ _ **c**	**K**	**[k]**	Un par**c** *A park*	Un ar**c** *A bow*	Se**c** *Dry*
_ **cqu**	**K**	**[b]**	A**cqu**érir *To acquire*	Gre**cque** *Greek*	A**cqu**itter *To acquit*
_ _ _ **ct**	**KT**	**[kt]**	Dire**ct** *Direct*	Le ta**ct** *The tact*	Exa**ct** *Exact*
cc + e.i	**KS**	**[ks]**	Un a**cc**ent *An accent*	A**cc**élérer *To accelerate*	Le su**cc**ès *The success*
C + e.i	**S**	**[s]**	Le **c**iel *The sky*	Un **c**itron *A lemon*	**C**elle *This*
Ç + a.o.u	**S**	**[s]**	Un gar**ç**on *A boy*	**Ç**a *That*	Fran**ç**ois
_ _ _ **nc**	**/**		Blan**c** *White*	Un ban**c** *A bench*	Un tron**c** *A trunk*
_ _ _ **ct**	**/**		Le suspe**ct** *The suspect*	Un aspe**ct** *An aspect*	Le respe**ct** *The respect*
_ _ **c** _ _	**G**	**[g]**	Une se**c**onde *A second*	Le se**c**ond *The second*	

HARD C [k] SOFT C [s]

Listening 63: Focus on C

Ca – Ce – Cé – Cè – Ci – Co – Cu – Cr – Cen – Cun – Con – Cou – Caill – Cueil

Listening 64: C in words

Ca	**Ca**rrément	*Outright*	________
Ce	**Ce**ci	*This*	________
Cé	La **cé**ramique	*The ceramic*	________
Cè	Un ac**cè**s	*An access*	________
Ci	Un **ci**tron	*A lemon*	________
Co	La noix de **coco**	*The coconut*	________
Cu	Du **cu**rry	*Some curry*	________
Cr	**Cr**ier	*To scream*	________
Cen	**Cen**trer	*To center*	________
Cun	Cha**cun**	*Each*	________
Con	**Con**tre	*Against*	________
Cou	**Cou**rir	*To run*	________
Caill	Un **caill**ou	*A rock*	________
Cueil	Un cer**cueil**	*A coffin*	________

CH [ʃ]

Tongue: Middle of the tongue touches the palate
The air goes through: The mouth
Lips: Depends on the next sound

Ch _ _ _	**CH**	[ʃ]	**Ch**anter *To sing*	**Ch**anger *To change*	Une **ch**ambre *A room*
_ _ **ch** _	**CH**	[ʃ]	Sè**che** *Dry (f)*	Blan**che** *White (f)*	Une ta**che** *A stain*
Sch _ _	**CH**	[ʃ]	Un **sch**éma *A diagram*		
Ch _ _ _	**K**	**[k]**	**Ch**ris	**Ch**ristian	**Chr**étien *Christian*

Listening 65: Focus on CH
Cha – Ché – Chè – Chi – Chu – Chr – Chan – Chin – Chien – Chou – Choi – Chau

Listening 66: CH in words

Cha	**Cha**cun	*Each*	______
Ché	**Ché**rir	*To cherish*	______
Chè	**Che**rcher	*To search*	______
Chi	**Chi**poter	*To finger*	______
Chu	**Chu**choter	*To whisper*	______
Chr	**Chr**étien	*Christian*	______
Chan	**Chan**ter	*To sing*	______
Chin	Un **chin**chilla	*A chinchilla*	______
Chien	Un **chien**	*A dog*	______
Chou	Une **chou**croute	*A sauerkraut*	______
Choi	**Choi**sir	*To choose*	______
Chau	**Chau**de	*Hot (f)*	______

D [d]

Tongue: Tip of the tongue touches the upper front teeth
The air goes through: The mouth
Lips: Slightly stretched horizontally

D _ _ _ _	D	[d]	**D**oux *Sweet*	**D**onner *To give*	Une **d**ent *A tooth*
_ _ d _ _	D	[d]	Par**d**on *Pardon*	A**d**orer *To adore*	Un ra**d**ar *A radar*
_ _ dd _ _	D	[d]	Une a**dd**ition *A bill*	Du che**dd**ar *Some cheddar*	
_ _ _ _ d	/		Le pie**d** *The foot*	Gran**d** *Tall*	Sour**d** *Deaf*
_ _ _ _ d	T	[t]	Un gran**d** **a**rbre = Un gran **t**arbre *A tall tree*		

Listening 67: Focus on D
Da – De – Dé – Dè – Di – Do – Du – Den – Daim – Don – Dou – Doi – Dille – Dail – Deuil - Douille

Listening 68: D in words

Da	Un ra**da**r	*A radar*	____________
De	**De**dans	*Inside*	____________
Dé	**Dé**faire	*To undo*	____________
Dè	**De**rrière	*Behind*	____________
Di	Une ad**di**tion	*A bill*	____________
Do	Un **do**mino	*A domino*	____________
Du	**Du**r	*Hard*	____________
Den	Une **den**t	*A tooth*	____________
Daim	Un **daim**	*A deer*	____________
Don	Un **don**jon	*A dungeon*	____________
Dou	La **dou**ceur	*The sweetness*	____________
Doi	Le **doi**gt	*The finger*	____________
Dille	Une cé**dille**	*A cedilla*	____________
Dail	Un chan**dail**	*A cardigan*	____________
Deuil	Le **deuil**	*The grief*	____________
Douille	Une **douille**	*A socket*	____________

F – PH [f]

Tongue: Bottom of the mouth
The air goes through: The mouth
Lips: Almost closed

F _ _ _ _	**F**	**[f]**	**F**aire *To do / To make*	Une **fl**ûte *A flute*	**F**uir *To flee*
_ _ **f** _ _	**F**	**[f]**	Un en**f**ant *A child*	Ra**f**ler *To raid*	Un re**f**us *A refusal*
_ _ **ff** _ _	**F**	**[f]**	Une e**ff**et *An effect*	Un chi**ff**on *A rag*	**Eff**acer *To erase*
Vowel + **f**	**F**	**[f]**	Neu**f** *New*	Veu**f** *Widow*	Pensi**f** *Thoughtful*
Ph _ _ _	**F**	**[f]**	Un **ph**are *A lighthouse*	Un **ph**oque *A seal*	Un **ph**araon *A pharaoh*
_ _ **ph** _ _	**F**	**[f]**	Un triom**ph**e *A triumph*	Un télé**ph**one *A phone*	Le gra**ph**isme *The graphism*
r + **f**	**/**		Un cer**f** *A deer*	Un ner**f** *A nerve*	
_ _ _ _ **f**	**V**	**[v]**	Neu**f** **a**ns = Neu **v**ans *Nine years*		

F - PH [f]

Listening 69: Focus on F

Fa – Fe - Fé – Fè – Fi – Fo – Fu – Fr – Fl – Fan – Faim – Fon – Fou – Foi – Fau – Fille – Faill – Feuil – Fouill

Listening 70: F in words

Fa	La **fa**mille	*The family*	______
Fe	La **fe**nêtre	*The window*	______
Fé	Une **fé**e	*A fairy*	______
Fè	**Fai**re	*To do / To make*	______
Fi	**Fi**er	*Proud*	______
Fo	Une **fo**rêt	*A forest*	______
Fu	La **fu**reur	*The fury*	______
Fr	Le **fr**ein	*The brake*	______
Fl	Une **fl**ûte	*A flute*	______
Fan	Un en**fan**t	*A child*	______
Faim	La **faim**	*The hunger*	______
Fon	**Fon**der	*To found*	______
Fou	**Fou**rrer	*To stuff*	______
Foi	La **foie**	*The liver*	______
Fau	**Fau**x	*False*	______
Fille	Une **fille**	*A girl*	______
Faill	**Faill**ir	*To fail*	______
Feuil	Du cer**feuil**	*Some chervil*	______
Fouill	**Fouill**er	*To search for*	______

HARD G [g] SOFT G [ʒ]

HARD G

Tongue: Middle of the tongue touches the palate
The air goes through: The mouth
Lips: Almost closed

SOFT G

Tongue: Tip touches the palate, not the teeth
The air goes through: The mouth
Lips: Depends on the next sound

G + r.l	**G**	**[g]**	**Gr**ave *Serious*	**Gr**and *Tall*	Un **gl**and *An acorn*
G + a.o.u	**G**	**[g]**	Un **gâ**teau *A cake*	Un **go**rille *A gorilla*	Une ba**gue** *A ring*
_ _ **gg** _ _	**G**	**[g]**	Un le**gg**ing *A legging*	Le jo**gg**ing *The sweatpants*	Un tobo**gg**an *A toboggan*
_ _ _ **ing**	**G**	**[g]**	Un legg**ing** *A legging*	Le jogg**ing** *The sweatpants*	Un camp**ing** *A campsite*
_ _ **gg** _ _	**GJ**	**[gʒ]**	Su**gg**érer *To suggest*	Une su**gg**estion *A suggestion*	Su**gg**estif *Suggestive*
_ _ **gt** _ _	**T**	**[t]**	Lon**gt**emps *Longtime*	Vin**gt**ième *Twentieth*	Une vin**gt**aine *Twenty*
_ _ _ _ **g**	**/**		Le san**g** *The blood*	Le ran**g** *The rank*	Lon**g** *Long*
_ _ _ **gt**	**/**		Un doi**gt** *A finger*		
G + e.i	**J**	**[ʒ]**	Un nua**ge** *A cloud*	Le **gî**te *The lodge*	Chan**ger** *To change*

HARD G [g] SOFT G [ʒ]

Listening 71: Focus on G

Ga – Ge – Gé – Gè – Gi – Go – Gr – Gl – Gen – Gon – Gou – Gueil – Gouill

Listening 72: G in words

Ga	**Ga**rer	*To park*	________
Ge	Un **ge**nou	*A knee*	________
Gé	**Gé**rer	*To manage*	________
Gè	Il **gè**le	*It's freezing*	________
Gi	Un **gî**te	*A lodge*	________
Go	Un **go**rille	*A gorilla*	________
Gr	Un **gr**ain	*A grain*	________
Gl	**Gl**uant	*Slimy*	________
Gen	Le **gen**re	*The gender*	________
Gon	Une **gon**dole	*A gondola*	________
Gou	Un ra**goû**t	*A stew*	________
Gueil	L'or**gueil**	*The pride*	________
Gouill	Une gar**gouill**e	*A gargoyle*	________

J [ʒ]

Tongue: Tip touches the palate, not the teeth
The air goes through: The mouth
Lips: Depends on the next sound

J _ _ _ _	J	[ʒ]	**J**eudi *Thursday*	Un **j**ouet *A toy*	Un **j**our *A day*
_ _ j _ _	J	[ʒ]	Bon**j**our *Hello*	A**j**ourner *To adjourn*	Ma**j**eur *Major*

Listening 73: Focus on J
Ja – Je – Ji – Jo – Ju – Jeu – Jui – Joi – Jun

Listening 74: J in words

Ja	**Ja**mais	*Never*	________
Je	Un **je**ton	*A token*	________
Ji	Une ta**ji**ne	*A tajine*	________
Jo	**Jo**vial	*Jovial*	________
Ju	Le **ju**do	*The judo*	________
Jeu	**Jeu**di	*Thursday*	________
Jui	**Jui**llet	*July*	________
Joi	La **joi**e	*The joy*	________
Jun	La **jun**gle	*The jungle*	________

H

H muet	Vowel	L'**h**abit *The piece of clothing*	L'**h**aleine *The breath*	L'**h**irondelle *The swallow*
H muet	Vowel	Un **h**abit *A piece of clothing*	Une **h**aleine *A breath*	Une **h**irondelle *A swallow*
H aspiré	Consonant	Le **h**ibou *The owl*	**H**aut *High*	Le **h**aricot *The bean*
H aspiré	Consonant	Un **h**ibou *An owl*	**H**aut *High*	Un **h**aricot *A bean*
_ _ **h** _ _	/	De**h**ors *Outside*	Un vé**h**icule *A vehicle*	Un sou**h**ait *A wish*

Listening 75: H aspiré in words

Le **h**ibou	*The owl*	________
Le **h**aricot	*The bean*	________
Le **h**érisson	*The hedgehog*	________
Le **h**amburger	*The hamburger*	________
La **h**auteur	*The height*	________
La **h**anche	*The hip*	________
Le **h**andicap	*The handicap*	________
La **H**ollande	*The Netherlands*	________

Listening 76: H muet in words

L'**h**irondelle	*The swallow*	________
L'**h**élicoptère	*The helicopter*	________
L'**h**éroïne	*The heroin*	________
L'**h**abitude	*The habit*	________
L'**h**istoire	*The story*	________
L'**h**iver	*The winter*	________
L'**h**orreur	*The horror*	________
L'**h**onneur	*The honor*	________

K - Q [k]

Tongue: Middle of the tongue touches the palate
The air goes through: The mouth
Lips: Slightly stretched horizontally

K _ _ _ _	**K**	**[k]**	Un **k**ilo *A kilo*	Un **k**it *A kit*	Un **k**angourou *A kangaroo*
_ _ _ _ k	**K**	**[k]**	Un kaya**k** *A kayak*	Un wo**k** *A wok*	Un anora**k** *An anorak*
Qu _ _ _	**K**	**[k]**	**Qu**and *When*	Un **qu**ai *A platform*	**Qu**oi *What*
_ _ _ qu _	**K**	**[k]**	La li**qu**eur *The liquor*	Le cir**que** *The circus*	Cha**que** *Each*
_ _ _ _ q	**K**	**[k]**	Cin**q** *Five*	Le co**q** *The rooster*	
_ _ _ _ q	**K**	**[k]**	Cin**q a**ns = Cin **k**ans *Five years*		

Listening 77: Focus on K
Ka – Ke – Ké – Kè – Ki – Ko – Ku – Kan – Kin – Koi – Keu

Listening 78: D in words

Ka	Un **ka**yak	*A kayak*	________
Ke	**Que**	*That*	________
Ké	Un karao**ké**	*A karaoke*	________
Kè	**Que**lle	*Which (f)*	________
Ki	Un **ki**lo	*A kilo*	________
Ko	Un **ko**ala	*A koala*	________
Ku	Un sudo**ku**	*A sudoku*	________
Kan	**Quan**d	*When*	________
Kin	Un re**quin**	*A shark*	________
Koi	**Quoi**	*What*	________
Keu	La li**queu**r	*The liquor*	________

L [l]

Tongue: Top of the tongue touches the upper front teeth
The air goes through: The mouth
Lips: Depends on the next sound

L _ _ _ _	L	[l]	**L**arge *Large*	**L**ent *Slow*	La **l**umière *The light*
_ _ ll _ _	L	[l]	Le ba**ll**et *The ballet*	La co**ll**e *The glue*	La canne**ll**e *The cinnamon*
_ _ ille	L	[l]	Une v**ille** *A city*	M**ille** *Thousand*	Tranqu**ille** *Quiet*
Ill _ _ _	L	[l]	**Ill**imité *Unlimited*	**Ill**égal *Illegal*	Une **ill**usion *An illusion*

Listening 79: Focus on L
La – Le – Lé – Lè – Li – Lo – Lu – Len – Lein – Lon – Lien – Lou – Loi – Leil

Listening 80: L in words

La	**La**ver	*To wash*	________
Le	**Le**ver	*To get up*	________
Lé	**Lé**gal	*Legal*	________
Lè	La **le**ssive	*The laundry soap*	________
Li	**Li**re	*To read*	________
Lo	Le **lo**t	*The lot*	________
Lu	La **lu**ne	*The moon*	________
Len	La **len**teur	*The slowness*	________
Lein	P**lein**	*Full*	________
Lon	**Lon**gue	*Long (f)*	________
Lien	Un **lien**	*A link*	________
Lou	Le **lou**p	*The wolf*	________
Loi	La **loi**	*The law*	________
Leil	Le so**leil**	*The sun*	________

M [m]

Tongue: Bottom of the mouth
The air goes through: The mouth
Lips: Open to close – From inside to outside

M _ _ _ _	M	[m]	**M**ercredi *Wednesday*	**M**anger *To eat*	Un **m**iroir *A mirror*
_ _ m _ _	M	[m]	Char**m**ant *Charming*	Une ca**m**éra *A camera*	Une plu**m**e *A feather*
_ _ mm _	M	[m]	Une po**mm**e *An apple*	Une so**mm**e *A sum*	Un gra**mm**e *A gram*
_ _ _ um	EM	[œm]	Un for**um** *A forum*	Maxim**um** *Maximum*	De l'opi**um** *Some opium*

Listening 81: Focus on M
Ma – Me – Mé – Mè – Mi – Mo – Mu – Men – Mun – Mon – Mien – Mou – Mill – Mail – Meil – Mouill

Listening 82: M in words

Ma	Un **ma**ri	*A husband*	____________
Me	**Me**	*Me*	____________
Mé	La **mé**téo	*The weather forecast*	____________
Mè	**Mai**s	*But*	____________
Mi	Une **mi**ette	*A crumb*	____________
Mo	Un **mo**rceau	*A piece*	____________
Mu	Un **mu**r	*A wall*	____________
Men	**Men**tir	*To lie*	____________
Mun	Com**mun**	*Common*	____________
Mon	Un **mon**t	*A mont*	____________
Mien	**Mien**	*Mine*	____________
Mou	**Mou**	*Soft*	____________
Mill	La fa**mill**e	*The family*	____________
Mail	L'é**mail**	*The enamel*	____________
Meil	Le ver**meil**	*The vermeil*	____________
Mouill	**Mouill**er	*To wet*	____________

N - GN [n] - [ɲ] - [ŋ]

Tongue: Top of the tongue touches the upper front teeth
The air goes through: The mouth
Lips: Depends on the next sound

N _ _ _ _	**N**	**[n]**	La **n**eige *The snow*	**N**oir *Black*	Un **n**avet *A turnip*
_ _ **nn** _ _	**N**	**[n]**	Une a**nn**ée *A year*	Bo**nn**e *Good (f)*	Do**nn**er *To give*
_ _ _ _ **n**	**N**	**[n]**	U**n** **a**vion = Un **n**avion *A plane*		
gn + oi	**N**	**[n]**	Une bai**gnoi**re *A bathtub*	Un pei**gnoi**r *A bathrobe*	
_ _ **gn** _ _	**NI**	**[ɲ]**	Un a**gn**eau *A lamb*	Un compa**gn**on *A companion*	Un champi**gn**on *A mushroom*
_ _ _ _ **ng**	**N**	**[ŋ]**	Un smok**ing** *A smoking*	Un park**ing** *A parking*	Un camp**ing** *A camping*

N - GN   [n] - [ɲ] - [ŋ]

Listening 83: Focus on N
Na – Ne – Né – Nè – Ni – No – Nu – Noi – Nain – Neu – Non – Nou – Nau – Nill – Naill - Nouill

Listening 84: N in words

Na	**Na**tif	*Native*	________
Ne	**Ne**	*(Part of negation)*	________
Né	Un **nez**	*A nose*	________
Nè	**Naî**tre	*To be born*	________
Ni	Le **ni**trogène	*The nitrogen*	________
No	Une **no**tice	*A manual*	________
Nu	**Nu**	*Naked*	________
Noi	**Noi**r	*Black*	________
Nain	Un **nain**	*A dwarf*	________
Neu	Un p**neu**	*A tire*	________
Non	**Non**	*No*	________
Nou	La **nounou**	*The nanny*	________
Nau	La **nau**sée	*The nausea*	________
Nill	La va**nill**e	*The vanilla*	________
Naill	Une te**naill**e	*A pliers*	________
Nouill	Les **nouill**es	*The noodles*	________

Listening 85: Focus on GN
Gna – Gné – Gnè – Gno – Gneau – Gnon

Listening 86: GN in words

Gna	Un si**gna**l	*A signal*	________
Gna	Une si**gna**ture	*A signature*	________
Gné	Une arai**gné**e	*A spider*	________
Gné	Ga**gner**	*To win*	________
Gnè	Un poi**gnet**	*A wrist*	________
Gno	Un vi**gno**ble	*A vineyard*	________
Gneau	Un a**gneau**	*A lamb*	________
Gnon	Un compa**gnon**	*A companion*	________
Gnon	Un champi**gnon**	*A mushroom*	________

P [p]

Tongue: Middle of the tongue touches the palate
The air goes through: The mouth
Lips: open to close – From inside to outside

P _ _ _ _	**P**	**[p]**	**P**ourquoi *Why*	**P**ar *By*	Une **p**iscine *A pool*
_ _ **p** _ _	**P**	**[p]**	Ram**p**er *To crawl*	La sou**p**e *The soup*	Une lou**p**e *A magnifying glass*
_ _ **pp** _ _	**P**	**[p]**	Un a**pp**ort *An input*	Une na**pp**e *A tablecloth*	Une gri**pp**e *A flu*
_ _ _ _ **p**	**P**	**[p]**	To**p** *Top*	Sto**p** *Stop*	Le ra**p** *The rap*
_ _ **pt** _ _	**PT**	**[pt]**	Un sym**pt**ôme *A symptom*	Som**pt**ueux *Sumptuous*	Dom**pt**er *To tame*
_ _ _ _ **p**	**/**		Tro**p** *Too much / many*	Un dra**p** *A sheet*	Un cam**p** *A camp*
_ _ **mpt** _	**/**		Co**mpt**er *To count*	Un aco**mpt**e *An account*	Un co**mpt**able *An accountant*

P [p]

Listening 87: Focus on P

Pa – Pe – Pé – Pè – Pi – Po – Pu – Pr – Pl – Pen – Pin – Pon – Pou – Poi – Peau – Pill – Paill

Listening 88: P in words

Pa	**Pa**raître	*To seem*	________
Pe	**Pe**tit	*Small*	________
Pé	**Pé**rir	*To perish*	________
Pè	Une **pe**lle	*A shovel*	________
Pi	La **pi**scine	*The pool*	________
Po	La **po**terie	*The pottery*	________
Pu	**Pu**er	*To stink*	________
Pr	**Pr**endre	*To take*	________
Pl	**Pl**aindre	*To complain*	________
Pen	**Pen**dre	*To hang*	________
Pin	Un **pin**	*A pine tree*	________
Pon	**Pon**dre	*To lay*	________
Pou	La **pou**dre	*The powder*	________
Poi	Le **poi**ds	*The weight*	________
Peau	Le cha**peau**	*The hat*	________
Pill	La pu**pill**e	*The pupil*	________
Paill	Une **paill**e	*A straw*	________

R [r]

Tongue: Bottom of the mouth
The air goes through: The mouth
Lips: Slightly stretched horizontally

The **sound R** in French is very different than the English one. The English one comes from the middle of the mouth, while the **French R** comes from the throat. It's similar to a gargling sound.
Note that in the IPA, the letter R can also be represented as [R] or [ʁ].

A good way to practice R in French is by putting a pencil between your teeth. Doing so will keep your tongue at the back of your mouth and force you to pronounce R from your throat.

The next step is to practice words with a consonant before the R:

Un **br**as	*An arm*
Un **cr**édit	*A credit*
Crier	*To scream*
Droit	*Right*
Franc	*Frank*
Prêt	*Ready*
Très	*Very*
Vrai	*True*

Then practice words starting with R:

Rond	*Round*
Une **r**ose	*A rose*
Rater	*To fail*
Rester	*To stay*
Refaire	*To redo*
La **r**ue	*The street*
Un **r**oi	*A king*
Rentrer	*To return*

R [r]

Tongue: Bottom of the mouth
The air goes through: The mouth
Lips: Slightly stretched horizontally

R _ _ _ _	**R**	**[r]**	**R**entrer *To return*	**R**evenir *To come back*	**R**ose *Pink*
_ _ rr _ _	**R**	**[r]**	Un a**rr**êt *A stop*	Un ve**rr**e *A glass*	Un se**rr**e *A greenhouse*
_ _ _ _ r	**R**	**[r]**	Che**r** *Dear*	La me**r** *The sea*	Pa**r** *By*
_ _ _ _ r	**R**	**[r]**	Le premie**r** **e**nfant = Le premié **r**enfant *The first child*		

Listening 89: Focus on R
Ra – Re – Ré – Rê – Ri – Ro – Ru – Ren - Ron – Rien – Rou – Roi – Reau – Rill – Rail – Reil – Reuil - Rouill

Listening 90: R in words

Ra	Un **râ**teau	*A rake*	______
Re	Un **re**quin	*A shark*	______
Ré	Un **ré**cital	*A concert*	______
Rè	Un **rê**ve	*A dream*	______
Ri	**Ri**re	*To laugh*	______
Ro	Une **ro**se	*A rose*	______
Ru	**Ru**stique	*Rustic*	______
Ren	**Ren**dre	*To give back*	______
Ron	Un **ron**d	*A circle*	______
Rien	**Rien**	*Nothing*	______
Rou	**Rou**ler	*To roll*	______
Roi	Un **roi**	*A king*	______
Reau	Un tau**reau**	*A bull*	______
Rill	Une g**rille**	*A grid*	______
Rail	Un **rail**	*A rail*	______
Reil	Pa**reil**	*Same*	______
Reuil	Un t**reuil**	*A hoist*	______
Rouill	**Rouill**er	*To rust*	______

S - Z [s] – [z]

Tongue: Tip touches the palate, not the teeth
The air goes through: The mouth
Lips: Depends on the next sound

S _ _ _ _	**S**	**[s]**	Le **s**ilence *The silence*	Un **s**avon *A soap*	Le **s**ucre *The sugar*
_ _ s _ _	**S**	**[s]**	Ab**s**ent *Absent*	En**s**emble *Together*	Un pa**s**teur *A pastor*
_ _ ss _ _	**S**	**[s]**	Un poi**ss**on *A fish*	La cui**ss**on *The cooking*	Cha**ss**er *To hunt*
_ _ _ _ s	**S**	**[s]**	Un our**s** *A bear*	Un sen**s** *A sense*	Un viru**s** *A virus*
_ _ sc _ _	**S**	**[s]**	De**sc**endre *To go down*	Une pi**sc**ine *A pool*	Un a**sc**enseur *An elevator*
_ _ z _ _	**S**	**[s]**	Les A**z**tèques *The Aztecs*		
Sc _ _ _	**SK**	**[sk]**	Un **sc**andale *A scandal*	Un **sc**ore *A score*	Un **sc**orpion *A scorpion*
S *between 2 vowels*	**Z**	**[z]**	Une mai**s**on *A house*	Une télévi**s**ion *A television*	Une chai**s**e *A chair*
Z _ _ _ _	**Z**	**[z]**	Un **z**èbre *A zebra*	Un **z**oom *A zoom*	Du **z**este *Some zest*
_ _ z _ _	**Z**	**[z]**	On**z**e *Eleven*	Trei**z**e *Thirteen*	Quin**z**e *Fifteen*
_ _ _ _ z	**Z**	**[z]**	Che**z** **e**ux = chez **z**eux *At their place*		
_ _ _ _ s	**Z**	**[z]**	Te**s** **a**ffaires = Tes **z**affaires *Your stuff*		
_ _ _ _ s	**/**		Toujour**s** *Always*	Aprè**s** *After*	Le ba**s** *The bottom*

S - Z [s] - [z]

Listening 91: Focus on S [s]

Sa – Se – Sé – Sè – Si – So - Su – Sen – Sein – Son – Sien – Sou – Soi – Seau – Sill – Seil – Seuil – Souill

Listening 92: S [s] in words

Sa	Il pas**sa**	*He went by*	________
Se	Elle **se**ra	*She will be*	________
Sé	As**sez**	*Enough*	________
Sè	Il **sai**t	*He knows*	________
Si	Une **si**rène	*A siren*	________
So	**So**rtir	*To leave*	________
Su	**Su**r	*On*	________
Sen	**Sen**tir	*To smell*	________
Sein	Un **sein**	*A breast*	________
Son	**Son**ger	*To think*	________
Sien	**Sien**	*His / Hers / Its*	________
Sou	**Sou**dre	*To solder*	________
Soi	Une **soi**rée	*An evening*	________
Seau	Un **seau**	*A bucket*	________
Sill	Un **sill**age	*A wake*	________
Seil	Un con**seil**	*An advice*	________
Seuil	Un **seuil**	*A doorstep*	________
Souill	**Souill**er	*To soil*	________

Listening 93: Focus on Z [z]

Za – Zé – Zè – Zi – Zo – Zu – Zan – Zon – Zeau – Zaill - Zeill

Listening 94: Z [z] in words

Za	Il ra**sa**	*He shaved*	________
Zé	**Zé**ro	*Zero*	________
Zè	Il pe**sai**t	*He weighted*	________
Zi	Une télévi**si**on	*A television*	________
Zo	Un **zoo**	*A zoo*	________
Zu	**Zu**t		________
Zan	Pe**san**t	*Heavy*	________
Zon	Une mai**son**	*A house*	________
Zeau	Un ré**seau**	*A network*	________
Zaill	La gri**saill**e	*The gloom*	________
Zeill	La gro**seill**e	*The redcurrant*	________

T [t] – [s]

Tongue: Tip of the tongue touches the upper front teeth
The air goes through: The mouth
Lips: Depends on the next sound

T _ _ _ _	**T**	**[t]**	**T**out *All*	**T**ard *Late*	Une **t**arte *Une tarte*
Th _ _ _	**T**	**[t]**	**T**homas	Un **th**é *A tea*	
_ _ **tt** _ _	**T**	**[t]**	Ba**tt**re *To beat*	Me**tt**re *To put*	Une pa**tt**e *A paw*
_ _ _ **tie**	**T**	**[t]**	La sor**tie** *The exit*	Une dynas**tie** *A dynasty*	La répar**tie** *The retort*
_ _ _ _ **t**	**T**	**[t]**	Ma**t** *Mat*	Ne**t** *Net*	Un bu**t** *A goal*
_ _ _ _ **t**	**T**	**[t]**	Tou**t un** = Tou **t**un *Whole*		
_ _ _ _ **t**	**/**		Tout *All*	Un bou**t** *A piece*	Une par**t** *A part*
_ _ **tion**	**S**	**[s]**	Atten**tion** *Attention*	Une récréa**tion** *A recess*	Une ac**tion** *An action*
_ **tien** _	**S**	**[s]**	Un pa**tient** *A patient*	La pa**tien**ce *The patience*	

T [t] – [s]

Listening 95: Focus on T

Ta – Te – Té – Tê – Ti – To – Tu – Tr – Ten – Tein – Ton – Tou – Toi – Teau – Till – Tail – Teil – Teuil – Touill

Listening 96: T in words

Ta	Une **tar**te	*A pie*	______
Te	**Te**	*You*	______
Té	Une **té**lévision	*A television*	______
Tê	Une **tê**te	*A head*	______
Ti	Par**ti**r	*To leave*	______
To	**Tô**t	*Early*	______
Tu	Un **tutu**	*A tutu*	______
Tr	**Tr**ier	*To sort*	______
Ten	**Ten**dre	*To stretch*	______
Tein	**Tein**dre	*To dye*	______
Ton	**Ton**dre	*To shave*	______
Tien	**Tien**	*Yours*	______
Tou	**Tou**te	*All (f)*	______
Toi	La **toi**ture	*The roof*	______
Teau	Le po**teau**	*The pole*	______
Till	Ti**till**er	*To tickle*	______
Tail	Un éven**tail**	*A range*	______
Teil	Un or**teil**	*A toe*	______
Teuil	Un fau**teuil**	*An armchair*	______
Touill	**Touill**er	*To toss*	______

V -W [v]

Tongue: Bottom of the mouth
The air goes through: The mouth
Lips: Almost closed

V_ _ _ _	V	[v]	**V**endre *To sell*	**V**enir *To come*	**V**ert *Green*
_ _ v _ _	V	[v]	Un sou**v**enir *A souvenir*	Sou**v**ent *Often*	La**v**er *To wash*
W_ _ _ _	V	[v]	Un **w**agon *A train car*		
_ _ _ _f	V	[v]	Neu**f a**ns = Neu **v**ans *Nine years*		

Listening 97: Focus on V
Va – Ve – Vé – Vè – Vi – Vo – Vu – Vr – Ven – Vin – Von – Vien – Vou – Voi – Veau – Vail – Veill

Listening 98: V in words

Va	**Va**rier	*To vary*	________
Ve	**Ve**nir	*To come*	________
Vé	**Vé**rifier	*To verify*	________
Vè	**Ve**rt	*Green*	________
Vi	**Vi**vre	*To live*	________
Vo	**Vo**tre	*Your*	________
Vu	**Vu**	*Seen*	________
Vr	**Vr**ai	*True*	________
Ven	**Ven**dre	*To sell*	________
Vin	**Vin**gt	*Twenty*	________
Von	Un sa**von**	*A soap*	________
Vien	**Vien**s	*Come*	________
Vou	**Vou**loir	*To want*	________
Voi	**Voi**r	*To see*	________
Veau	Un **veau**	*A veal*	________
Vail	Un tra**vail**	*A job*	________
Veill	**Veill**er	*To ensure*	________

W [w]

Tongue: Bottom of the mouth
The air goes through: The mouth
Lips: Rounded

W _ _ _ _	**W**	**[w]**	Un **w**att *A watt*	Le **w**eb *The web*	Le **w**ifi *The wifi*
_ _ w _ _	**W**	**[w]**	Le R**w**anda *Rwanda*		

X [gz] – [ks] – [z] – [s]

Tongue: Tip touches the palate, not the teeth
The air goes through: The mouth
Lips: Slightly stretched horizontally

X _ _ _ _	**GZ**	**[gz]**	**X**avier	Un **x**ylophone *A xylophone*	
X *Before a vowel*	**GZ**	**[gz]**	Un e**x**emple *An example*	E**x**iler *To exile*	E**x**ister *To exist*
X *Before a consonant*	**KS**	**[ks]**	Un te**x**te *A text*	E**x**primer *To express*	Un e**x**tra *An extra*
X *In numbers*	**Z**	**[z]**	Deu**x**ième *Second*	Di**x**ième *Tenth*	
_ _ _ _ x	**Z**	**[z]**	Deu**x** **a**ns = Deu **z**ans *Two years*		
_ _ _ _ x	**/**		Deu**x** *Two*	Un choi**x** *A choice*	Le pri**x** *The price*
_ _ _ _ x	**S**	**[s]**	Di**x** *Ten*	Si**x** *Six*	

UNUSUAL PRONUNCIATION

Listening 99: Unusual pronunciation

When OI is pronounced O:

OI _ _ _	**O**	**[ɔ]**	Un **oi**gnon *An onion*		

When E is pronounced A:

_ _ e _ _	**A**	**[a]**	Une f**e**mme *A woman*	Évid**e**mment *Obviously*	Innoc**e**mment *Innocently*
			Intellig**e**mment *Intelligently*	Prud**e**mment *Carefully*	Viol**e**mment *Violently*

When AI is pronounced E:

_ _ AI _ _	**E**	**[ə]**	Nous f**ai**sons *We do*	Je f**ai**sais *I did*	Tu f**ai**sais *You did*
			Il f**ai**sait *He did*	Elle f**ai**sait *She did*	Vous f**ai**siez *You did*
			Ils f**ai**saient *They did*	Elle f**ai**saient *They did*	

When U is pronounced as a closed EU:

_ _ u _ _	**EU**	**[œ]**	Un p**u**zzle *A puzzle*		

When ON is pronounced E:

_ _ on _ _	**E**	**[ə]**	M**on**sieur *Sir*		

When O and N are pronounced distinctly in ON:

_ _ on _ _	**O-N**	**[ɔn]**	Un b**on**homme *A little boy*	Un b**on**homme de neige *A snowman*	

When the final S is pronounced:

_ _ _ _ s	**S**	**[s]**	Un our**s** *A bear*	Un viru**s** *A virus*	Un tournevi**s** *A screwdriver*

UNUSUAL PRONUNCIATION

_ _ _ _ s	**S**	**[s]**	Un utéru**s** *A uterus*	Un péni**s** *A penis*	Le tenni**s** *The tennis*
			Un fil**s** *A son*	Un rhinocéro**s** *A rhinoceros*	Du couscou**s** *Some couscous*

When the final T is pronounced:

_ _ _ _ t	**T**	**[t]**	Ma**t** *Mat*	Ne**t** *Net*	Un bu**t** *A goal*

When PT is pronounced T:

_ _ _ pt	**T**	**[t]**	Se**pt** *Seven*	Com**pt**er *To count*	Un com**pt**able *An accountant*

When MN is pronounced N:

_ _ mn _	**N**	**[n]**	L'auto**mn**e *Fall / Autumn*	Conda**mn**er *To convict*

When AI is pronounced É and È:

Ai _ _ _	**É**	**[e]**	**Ai**mer *To like / To love*		
Ai _ _ _	**È**	**[ɛ]**	J'**ai**me *I like / I love*	Tu **ai**mes *You like / You love*	Il **ai**me *He likes / He loves*

When EN is pronounced IN:

_ _ _ en	**IN**	**[ɛ̃]**	Un exam**en** *An exam*

When C is pronounced G:

_ _ c _ _	**G**	**[g]**	Une se**c**onde *A second*	Se**c**ond(e) *Second*

When AON is pronounced AN:

_ _ aon	**AN**	**[ɑ̃]**	Un f**aon** *A fawn*	Un t**aon** *A horsefly*	Un p**aon** *A peacock*

UNUSUAL PRONUNCIATION

When UM is pronounced EM:

_ _ _ **um**	**EM**	**[œm]**	Un for**um** *A forum*	Maxim**um** *Maximum*	De l'opi**um** *Some opium*

When BS is pronounced PS:

_ _ **bs** _ _	**PS**	**[ps]**	A**bs**olument *Absolutely*	A**bs**ent *Absent*

AY in PAYS:

_ **ay** _	**A-I**	**[ɛi]**	Un p**ay**s *A country*

Words with 2 different pronunciations depending on the area:

_ _ _ _ **s**	**S - /**	**[s] - /**	Un anana**s** *A pineapple*	Un ananas *A pineapple*
_ _ _ _ **t**	**T - /**	**[t] - /**	Ving**t** *Twenty*	Vingt *Twenty*

Words with 2 different pronunciations and 2 different meanings:

_ _ _ _ **s**	**S - /**	**[s] - /**	Tou**s** *All*	Tous *All*
_ _ _ _ **s**	**S - /**	**[s] - /**	Plu**s** *More*	Plus *Not enough*

Irregular plurals:

Un **œu**f *An egg*	**[œ]**	Des **œu**fs *Some eggs*	**[ø]**
Un b**œu**f *Beef / A bull*	**[œ]**	Des b**œu**fs *Beef / Bulls*	**[ø]**
Un **œil** *An eye*	**[œj]**	Des **yeu**x *Eyes*	**[jø]**
Un **os** *A bone*	**[ɔs]**	Des **o**s *Bones*	**[o]**

WORD STRESS

The French stress is barely noticeable. While it is present on the last syllable of each word (besides one-syllable words) and each sentence, it's easy to miss.

French is what we call a "**syllable-timed language**" which means that each syllable has to be pronounced the same length. It's very different from English, which is a "**stress-timed language**".

The stress in English can fall on any syllable.
Let's have a look at a word used in English and in French:

If you ever wonder why French people don't add any stress while speaking English, this is why.

- English: Imagination
- French: Imagina**tion**

Like I said, the stress is hard to hear in French. I always say, at the beginning, instead of worrying about adding the stress correctly, try to not add any stress. It will be closer to the real pronunciation.

The stress that you should absolutely add is what is called "the inflection" added by a question mark.

- Tu es au bureau.
- Tu es au bur**eau** ?

- Il habite à Vancouver.
- Il habite à Vancou**ver** ?

FRENCH READING PRACTICE 1

Listen to the recordings, try to find the silent letters, links and identify the different sounds. You can find the answer next page.

Listening 100: French Reading Practice 1 - Slow pace
Listening 101: French Reading Practice 1 - Normal pace

LE PRINTEMPS - *Spring*

Le printemps est une des quatre saisons de l'année, juste après l'hiver et avant l'été. Cette saison commence le 30 mars et se termine le 30 juin. Mais les dates peuvent changer selon les régions du monde. En français, on dit que le printemps est la saison des amours. C'est le moment où les oiseaux s'accouplent, les fleurs poussent, et les arbres redeviennent verts.

Le printemps est une des quatre saisons de l'année, juste après l'hiver et avant l'été. Cette saison commence le 30 mars et se termine le 30 juin. Mais les dates peuvent changer selon les régions du monde. En français, on dit que le printemps est la saison des amours. C'est le moment où les oiseaux s'accouplent, les fleurs poussent, et les arbres redeviennent verts.

FIND THE SILENT LETTERS AND THE LINKS

Le printemps est une des quatre saisons de l'année, juste après l'hiver et avant l'été. Cette saison commence le 30 mars et se termine le 30 juin. Mais les dates peuvent changer selon les régions du monde. En français, on dit que le printemps est la saison des amours. C'est le moment où les oiseaux s'accouplent, les fleurs poussent, et les arbres redeviennent verts.

IDENTIFY THE DIFFERENT **SOUNDS**

Le printemps est une des quatre saisons de l'année, juste après l'hiver et avant l'été. Cette

saison commence le 30 mars et se termine le 30 juin. Mais les dates peuvent changer selon

les régions du monde. En français, on dit que le printemps est la saison des amours. C'est le

moment où les oiseaux s'accouplent, les fleurs poussent, et les arbres redeviennent verts.

EXAMPLE : **Le** pr**in**te**m**ps **est** Tune ...

FRENCH READING PRACTICE 1

LE PRINTEMPS - *Spring*

Le printemps est une des quatre saisons de l'année, juste après l'hiver et avant l'été. Cette saison commence le 30 mars et se termine le 30 juin. Mais les dates peuvent changer selon les régions du monde. En français, on dit que le printemps est la saison des amours. C'est le moment où les oiseaux s'accouplent, les fleurs poussent, et les arbres redeviennent verts.

Le printemps est une des quatre saisons de l'année, juste après l'hiver et avant l'été. Cette saison commence le 30 mars et se termine le 30 juin. Mais les dates peuvent changer selon les régions du monde. En français, on dit que le printemps est la saison des amours. C'est le moment où les oiseaux s'accouplent, les fleurs poussent, et les arbres redeviennent verts.

FIND THE SILENT LETTERS AND THE LINKS

Le printemps est Tune des quatre saisons de l'année, juste après l'hiver et avant l'été. Cette saison commence le 30 mars et se termine le 30 juin. Mais les dates peuvent changer selon les régions du monde. En français, on dit que le printemps est la saison des Zamours. C'est le moment où les Zoiseaux s'accouplent, les fleurs poussent, et les Zarbres redeviennent verts.

IDENTIFY THE DIFFERENT **SOUNDS**

Le printemps **est** Tune **des** quatre **saison**s **de** l'année, juste après l'h**iver et avan**t l'été.
E EN È È ÈZON E È É EN

Cette **saison** commenc**e le** 30 mars **et se termin**e **le** 30 **juin**. **Mai**s **les** dates **peuv**ent
SÈ ÈZON ENS E É E È E WIN È È

ch**anger** sel**on les** régi**on**s du mond**e**. **En françai**s, **on** dit q**ue le printem**ps **est** la **saison** des
ENJÉ È J ENSÈ E E EN È ÈZON È

Zam**our**s. **C'est le momen**t **où les** Z**oiseau**x s'acc**oupl**ent, **les** fleurs **pouss**ent, **et les** Zarbres
SÈ E È ZWAZo È É È

redeviennent ver**ts**.
E E È È

FRENCH READING PRACTICE 2

Listen to the recordings, try to find the silent letters, links and identify the different sounds. You can find the answer next page.

Listening 102: French Reading Practice 2 - Slow pace
Listening 103: French Reading Practice 2 - Normal pace

MA JOURNÉE IDÉALE - *My ideal day*

Ma journée idéale est une journée sans responsabilités ni horaire. Me lever à l'heure que je veux, manger quand j'en ai envie et me coucher quand je suis fatigué(e).
Si le temps le permet, j'irais faire une randonnée en montagne, admirer le coucher de soleil, partager un bon repas avec ma famille et terminer la soirée autour d'un feu de bois. Et vous, quelle serait votre journée idéale ?

My ideal day is a day without any responsibilities or schedule. I would be able to get up when I want, eat when I feel like it and sleep when I'm tired. If the weather is nice, I would go for a hike in the mountains, watch the sunset, have a nice meal with my family and end the evening around a campfire. And you, what would your ideal day be like?

FIND THE SILENT LETTERS AND THE LINKS

Ma journée idéale est une journée sans responsabilités ni horaire. Me lever à l'heure que je veux, manger quand j'en ai envie et me coucher quand je suis fatigué(e).
Si le temps le permet, j'irais faire une randonnée en montagne, admirer le coucher de soleil, partager un bon repas avec ma famille et terminer la soirée autour d'un feu de bois. Et vous, quelle serait votre journée idéale ?

IDENTIFY THE DIFFERENT **SOUNDS**

Ma journée idéale est une journée sans responsabilités ni horaire. Me lever à l'heure que je

veux, manger quand j'en ai envie et me coucher quand je suis fatigué(e).

Si le temps le permet, j'irais faire une randonnée en montagne, admirer le coucher de soleil,

partager un bon repas avec ma famille et terminer la soirée autour d'un feu de bois. Et vous,

quelle serait votre journée idéale ?

FRENCH READING PRACTICE 2

MA JOURNÉE IDÉALE - *My ideal day*

Ma journée idéale est une journée sans responsabilités ni horaire. Me lever à l'heure que je veux, manger quand j'en ai envie et me coucher quand je suis fatigué(e).
Si le temps le permet, j'irais faire une randonnée en montagne, admirer le coucher de soleil, partager un bon repas avec ma famille et terminer la soirée autour d'un feu de bois. Et vous, quelle serait votre journée idéale ?

My ideal day is a day without any responsibilities or schedule. I would be able to get up when I want, eat when I feel like it and sleep when I'm tired. If the weather is nice, I would go for a hike in the mountains, watch the sunset, have a nice meal with my family and end the evening around a campfire. And you, what would your ideal day be like?

FIND THE SILENT LETTERS AND THE LINKS

Ma journée idéale est Tune journée sans responsabilités ni horaire. Me lever à l'heure que je veux, manger quand j'en Nai envie et me coucher quand je suis fatigué(e).
Si le temps le permet, j'irais faire une randonnée en montagne, admirer le coucher de soleil, partager un bon repas avec ma famille et terminer la soirée autour d'un feu de bois. Et vous, quelle serait votre journée idéale ?

IDENTIFY THE DIFFERENT **SOUNDS**

Ma **jour**née idéale **est** Tune **jour**née **san**s **res**pon**s**abilités ni horaire. **Me lever** à l'heure que
È EN È È E E É E

je veux, **manger** quand **j'en** Nai **envi**e **et** me **coucher** quand **je sui**s fatigué(e).
E ENJÉ EN É É E É EN E

Si **le tem**ps **le** perme**t**, j'ir**ai**s **fair**e une **ran**donnée **en** mon**ta**gne, admir**er le** couch**er de**
E EN E È È È È EN É E É E

soleil, parta**ger un bon** repas avec ma fam**ill**e **et** ter**miner** la s**oir**ée **autour** d'**un feu de boi**s.
JÉ E É È É WA o E WA

Et vous, qu**ell**e **serai**t votre **jour**née idéale ?
É È E È

FRENCH READING PRACTICE 3

Listen to the recordings, try to find the silent letters, links and identify the different sounds. You can find the answer next page.

Listening 104: French Reading Practice 3 - Slow pace
Listening 105: French Reading Practice 3 - Normal pace

LE CANADA - *Canada*

Le Canada se situe en Amérique du Nord et partage sa frontière avec les États-Unis. Le Canada compte dix provinces et trois territoires fédéraux. Le pays vient de passer les trente-huit millions d'habitants. Il a été voté numéro 1 pour sa qualité de vie pour la cinquième année consécutive. Le Canada accueille environ 300.000 (trois-cents-mille) immigrants chaque année.

Canada is located in North America and shares a border with the United States. Canada has ten provinces and three federal territories. The country has just passed having thirty-eight million inhabitants. It was voted number one for quality of life for the fifth year in a row. Each year, Canada welcomes on average 300,000 immigrants.

FIND THE SILENT LETTERS AND THE LINKS

Le Canada se situe en Amérique du Nord et partage sa frontière avec les États-Unis. Le Canada compte dix provinces et trois territoires fédéraux. Le pays vient de passer les trente-huit millions d'habitants. Il a été voté numéro 1 pour sa qualité de vie pour la cinquième année consécutive. Le Canada accueille environ 300.000 (trois-cents-mille) immigrants chaque année.

IDENTIFY THE DIFFERENT **SOUNDS**

Le Canada se situe en Amérique du Nord et partage sa frontière avec les États-Unis. Le

Canada compte dix provinces et trois territoires fédéraux. Le pays vient de passer les trente-

huit millions d'habitants. Il a été voté numéro 1 pour sa qualité de vie pour la cinquième

année consécutive. Le Canada accueille environ 300.000 (trois-cents-mille) immigrants

chaque année.

FRENCH READING PRACTICE 3

LE CANADA - *Canada*

Le Canada se situe en Amérique du Nord et partage sa frontière avec les États-Unis. Le Canada compte dix provinces et trois territoires fédéraux. Le pays vient de passer les trente-huit millions d'habitants. Il a été voté numéro 1 pour sa qualité de vie pour la cinquième année consécutive. Le Canada accueille environ 300.000 (trois-cents-mille) immigrants chaque année.

Canada is located in North America and shares a border with the United States. Canada has ten provinces and three federal territories. The country has just passed having thirty-eight million inhabitants. It was voted number one for quality of life for the fifth year in a row. Each year, Canada welcomes on average 300,000 immigrants.

FIND THE SILENT LETTERS AND THE LINKS

Le Canada se situe en NAmérique du Nord et partage sa frontière avec les ZÉtats-ZUnis. Le Canada compte dix provinces et trois territoires fédéraux. Le pays vient de passer les trente-huit millions d'habitants. Il a été voté numéro 1 pour sa qualité de vie pour la cinquième année consécutive. Le Canada accueille environ 300.000 (trois-cents-mille) immigrants chaque année.

IDENTIFY THE DIFFERENT **SOUNDS**

Le Canada **se** situe **en** NAmérique du Nord **et** partag**e** sa fr**on**tière av**ec** l**es** ZÉtats-ZUnis. **Le**
E E É J È È E
Canada c**om**pte dix pr**o**v**inc**es **et** tr**oi**s terri**toi**res fédér**au**x. **Le** pa**y**s **vien**t **de** pass**er** l**es**
S É WA È WA o E È-I E É È
tren**t**e-h**uit** milli**on**s d'habit**an**ts. Il a été v**o**té numér**o** 1 p**our** sa qualité **de** vie **pour** la
O o E
cinquième année **con**sécutive. **Le** Canada ac**cueill**e **en**vir**on** 300.000 (tr**oi**s-**cen**ts-mille)
S E WA S
immigr**an**ts chaque année.
EN

Fin

Also by Dylane Moreau

Books including video lessons

The Complete French Pronunciation Course
The Complete French Conjugation Course
The Complete French Grammar Course
The Complete French Vocabulary Course (coming soon)
The Complete French Expressions Course (coming soon)

Vocabulary

1000 Most Common French Words
The Little French Dictionary Of Word Families

Stories

Dix Choses Que Je Fais Tous Les Jours – Ten Things I Do Every Day
Le Mois D'Avril – The Month Of April

Made in the USA
Las Vegas, NV
21 February 2025

18439219R00057